Windows Into Eternity

The Promise and the Plan
Volume 1

by Sue Rhineheimer

Copyright © 2004 by Sue Rhineheimer

Windows Into Eternity
by Sue Rhineheimer

Printed in the United States of America

ISBN 1-594676-63-1

All rights reserved solely by the author. The author guarantees all contents are original and do not infringe upon the legal rights of any other person or work. No part of this book may be reproduced in any form without the permission of the author. The views expressed in this book are not necessarily those of the publisher.

Unless otherwise indicated, Bible quotations are taken from the New International Version of the Bible. Copyright © 1973, 1978 and 1984 by Zondervan Publishing House.

www.xulonpress.com

Dedicated to My Best Friend,
My Husband,
Charles Rhineheimer

Acknowledgements:

My gratitude goes to the Ladies' Bible Classes at the Tri-City Church of Christ in Chandler, AZ and the Village Meadows Church of Christ in Sierra Vista, AZ for studying all of my rough drafts in such an enthusiastic manner, and especially to Nona Nix, my wonderful friend and confidant who encouraged me to have this put into print.

I am also grateful to all the dedicated Sunday School Teachers who taught me well while I was growing up including Mrs. Elna Brandenburg of Grandfalls, Texas, and John Prichard of Mesa, Arizona. In my adult life, I am thankful to the dedicated staff at the Sunset International Bible Institute for their teachings and examples, especially Gerald and Bobbie Paden.

Table of Contents:

Chapter 1
The Beginning,
    A Window to **Christ, the Word of God**............11

Chapter 2
Adam and Eve,
    A Window to **Christ and His Church**..............19

Chapter 3
The Covering for Sin,
    A Window to **Christ the Innocent Substitute**..29

Chapter 4
The Seed of Woman,
    A Window to **Christ the Victor over Death**.....37

Chapter 5
The Flood of Noah's Day,
    A Window into **A Warning of Coming Judgment**..45

Chapter 6
The Ark of Noah,
    A Window into the **church of Christ**.................55

Chapter 7
Three Promises to Abraham,
    A Window into **Promises Fulfilled** 63

Chapter 8
Melchizedek, King and Priest
    A Window to **Christ our King and Priest** 73

Chapter 9
Sarah and Hagar,
    A Window into the **Old and New Testaments** 81

Chapter 10
The Passover Lamb,
    A Window to **Christ the Lamb of God** 91

Chapter 11
The Blood of the Lamb,
    A Window into **Life or Death** 99

Chapter 12
The Unleavened Bread,
    A Window to the **Sinless Christ** 107

Chapter 13
Crossing The Red Sea,
    A Window into **Baptism: From Slavery to Freedom** 113

Chapter 1

THE BEGINNING
Christ, the Word of God

The divine identity of Jesus is firmly established in the Gospel of John. It reads much like the very first verse of the Bible. Jesus was no ordinary man.

- *In the beginning was the word, and the word was with God, and the word was God (John 1:1).*

Jesus has always been. From the very beginning of time, He was with God. He was and is the Word of God. He was and is the creator of all things; He was and is God Himself.

- *In the beginning God created the heavens and the earth (Genesis 1:1).*

God, in His great love, sent His Living Word, a part of Himself, into the world so that man could know Him. We know Him as Jesus Christ, the Son of God. However, there is much more to Jesus than being the Son of God.

Stunning illustrations of Christ, the Living Word of God,

can be found in the first chapter of John, in Colossians and in Hebrews. Let's look back in time through these windows.

In the Beginning Was the Word...
Jesus as God

- *<u>In the beginning was the Word</u> (John 1:1).*

Jesus existed with God and as God. Like God, He always has been, and always will be. He is not subject to the laws of time or space. Because He is God, He has the same attributes of God. He is omniscient, omnipotent, and omnipresent.

- *He is <u>before</u> all things... (Colossians 1:17).*

At the beginning of all things, Jesus was already there. Jesus is not a created being; He did not have a beginning. Jesus existed before time began. He is before all things.

The Word Was with God...
Jesus, the Creator

- *<u>For by him all things were created</u>: things in heaven and earth, visible and invisible, whether thrones or powers or rulers or authorities; <u>all things were created by him and for him</u> (Colossians 1:16).*
- *... <u>through whom he made the universe</u> (Hebrews 1:2).*

Jesus is the creator. As God spoke his powerful word, Jesus did the creating. He created all the things we see and all the things we do not see. As the powerful Word of God, the creation is His.

- *He is the <u>beginning</u> of all things (Colossians 1:18).*

The source of a river is where it begins. This "beginning," in Colossians 1:18, means that Jesus is the *source* or *origin* of all things. It is not a reference to *time*. All created things have their beginnings or their source in Christ. He is the "source" of eternal salvation for all who obey Him (Hebrews 5:8).

Jesus, the Sustainer of the Universe

- *...and in him <u>all things hold together</u> (Colossians 1:17).*
- *The son is the radiance of God's glory and the exact representation of his being, <u>sustaining all things by his powerful word</u> (Hebrews 1:3).*

Did you see the transit of Venus across the face of the sun? Do you know when it will happen again? Those who study these things know. They are able to calculate exactly when these things will occur, because all the laws of nature and creation are in compliance with the power of Jesus. All things in the universe operate under His complete control.

Without this authority over His creation, everything in the universe would immediately disintegrate. Watching the sun rise each morning, and seeing the stars in the same place each night, is visible proof that He is still in complete control. Simply put, He literally holds the universe together. Never minimize the importance of these verses!

The Word Was God

- *He is <u>the image of the invisible God</u>...(Colossians 1:15).*
- *For <u>God was pleased</u> to have <u>all his fullness</u> dwell in him (Colossians 1:19).*
- *Anyone who has <u>seen me has seen the Father</u> (John 14:9).*
- *The son is the <u>radiance of God's glory and the exact representation of his being</u>... (Hebrews 1:3).*

Jesus was indeed the very reflection of God in human form. If we want to know what God is like we need only to look at Jesus. To know His love, His goodness, His mercy, we look to Jesus. Everything God is, Jesus is. The whole essence of God is present in Jesus, and this greatly pleases God.

The Word Became Flesh

- *<u>The Word became flesh</u> and made his dwelling among us (John 1:14).*

The Living Word of God visited the earth in the form of man and lived as one of us. Greek mythology may allude to gods visiting the earth from time to time, but this visitation of our God transcended all that the human mind could ever imagine.

Jesus was called Immanuel, which means "God with us." Think of it, God came down to live as one of us.

Only an astounding act of love would compel Jesus Christ leave the glory of heaven and walk the earth as a mortal, subject to time, pain, and death. What love He has for you and me!

Jesus has All Authority

- *...the <u>firstborn</u> over all creation... (Colossians 1:15).*

In Jewish families the *firstborn son* received the double inheritance. The firstborn became the head of the family, the "authority." The extra money inherited was used to fulfill this responsibility and to care for the family.

- *...but in these last days he has spoken to us by his Son, whom he appointed <u>heir of all things</u>... (Hebrews 1:2).*

Jesus, as heir of all things, accepted the responsibility over all creation as the firstborn. The inheritance is His to be used to care for His family.

- *...the firstborn from the dead so that <u>in everything he might have the supremacy</u> (Colossians 1:18).*

Obviously, Christ was not the first to be raised from the dead. Both Elijah and Elisha raised children from the dead, and Jesus, himself, raised Jairus' daughter and Lazarus from the dead. However, all these people died again. Jesus became the firstborn from the dead by the fact that He never died again. Christ is the first to never die again. He lives forever. His resurrection from the dead is the proof of His supremacy.

- *<u>All authority is given to me</u> in heaven and on earth (Matthew 28:18).*

Who has the right to be in command of all creation, including mankind? Jesus was given that right by His Father in heaven. Jesus became the authority because He submitted to life here on earth, and to death on the cross for the sins of the entire world. His perfection came through suffering (Hebrews 2:10). He is the author and finisher of our faith (Hebrews 5:8). All authority belongs to Him.

Jesus, Head of the Church

- *And he is the head of the body, the church (Colossians 1:18).*

The church is the body of Christ. Just as our brain gives instruction to our body, Christ, as the head of his body the church, supplies us with instructions for Christian living. This makes us intricately connected to His wishes. Just as you cannot have a head without a body, neither can you have Christ without His church.

Jesus, the Reconciler

- *And through him to <u>reconcile</u> to himself all things, whether things on earth or things in heaven, <u>by making peace through his blood</u> shed on the cross (Colossians 1:20).*
- *Since we have now been justified by his blood, how much more shall we be saved from God's wrath through him. For if, when we were God's enemies, <u>we were reconciled to him through the death of his Son, how much more, having been reconciled, shall we be saved</u> through his life (Romans 5:9, 10).*

Reconciliation means to bring back together. Those reconciled are in the church, which is the body of Christ. Though our sins kept us separated from God, Christ brought us back to God through His death on the cross. Without His blood, we would deserve the wrath of God. He is the great Reconciler.

The Word is Coming Back

- *And if I go and prepare a place for you, <u>I will come back</u> and take you to be with me that you also may be where I am (John 14:3).*

Jesus reassured His disciples in the upper room that He would return to take them back with him to heaven. Jesus loves us so much He wants us to be with Him. He never tires of our presence and has made provisions for us to be with Him eternally. Make no mistake; He is coming again to take us home.

Conclusion

God's love for mankind was so great that He was willing to become one of us in order to show us the way to heaven. Unlike the gods of mythology, our God humbled Himself and become a man. He entered this world, not as a warrior, but as a baby, born of a virgin in a stable in Bethlehem. As a man, He did not ride into Jerusalem as a conquering king on a white horse, but as a Savior riding on a donkey, signifying that He was coming in peace.

The fact that God would become a man is probably the most amazing reality known. It is so astounding that many just do not believe it. There are some who accept the reality of an all-knowing and all-powerful God, but do not accept the reality that He entered this world as a human. It is shocking to think that the creator of all would allow Himself to be crucified by those He created. However, Jesus is the only way that we will ever be able to reach God, and to reject Him is the ultimate insult to Him who gave up so much for us.

- *I am the way, the truth, and the life. No man comes to the Father except through me (John 14:6).*

The God, who made us and loves us, became one of us, to show us the way home. When we look at Christ, we see the image of God.

Questions for discussion:
1. What three words begin the Old Testament and the book of John in the New Testament (Genesis 1:1; John 1:1)?
2. Using a Bible Dictionary, define omnipresent, omnipotent, and omniscient. Give examples of each from scripture.
3. Was Jesus created? How do you know?

4. How can Jesus be God and be with God at the same time? Explain.
5. What is the significance of the name Immanuel? Why do you think God became a man?
6. Name the miracles of Jesus that show His complete control of nature.
7. Using a Bible Encyclopedia explain the differences in the Birthright and the Blessings given usually to the firstborn son. Recall the story of Jacob and Esau.
8. Can we say we love Jesus and then neglect His church? Why or why not?
9. What verse would you refer to when talking with someone who tells you that all religions lead to God?
10. What was accomplished by Jesus' death on the cross (Romans 5:8,9,10)?

CHAPTER 2

ADAM AND EVE
Christ and His Church

The Creation of Man

God took special care in the creation of man, showing the significance of this creation over all others. God did not speak man into existence as He did the rest of creation. God's own hands intricately formed the man from the dust of the ground.

Even though the plants and animals were considered as living, God "breathed" into man the breath of life and the Bible says he became a "living being" or a living soul. Man was the ultimate creation, made with loving care and special attention. Of all living things, only man received the breath of God in his nostrils, and was given a spirit from God.

- *The LORD God said, "It is not good for man to be alone. I will make a helper suitable for him" (Genesis 2:18b).*

But man was alone. As Adam finished naming the

animals that God brought before him, one thing had become painfully obvious. There was no helper suitable for him. There was none like Adam in the animal world.

Of course, God knew of this, but Adam needed to know this fact firsthand. Adam was not complete by himself. He needed a helper suitable for him, a helpmeet. He had no helper who was like him. After establishing this truth in Adam's mind, God caused Adam to fall into a deep sleep, and then fashioned a woman from his rib.

- *...But for Adam no suitable helper was found. So the LORD God caused the man to fall into a deep sleep; and while he was sleeping, he took one of the man's ribs and closed up the place with flesh. Then the LORD God made a woman from the rib he had taken out of the man, and he brought her to the man (Genesis 2:20b-23).*

In the very first surgery, woman was made from Adam's rib.

The Creation of Woman

Woman, too, was an extraordinary creation. Her creation was also straight from the hand of God. However, she was not made directly from the dust, as was Adam. Woman was formed from the rib of Adam, as a part of him, yet separate from him. She was made to be his helper and his companion. She was made to assist him in his life's work.

Often in wedding vows, ministers make mention of this fact. They are fond of pointing out that woman was not made from the head of man that she might rule over him, nor from the foot of man that he might tread on her; but from his side that she might stand beside him and be protected by him.

The Institution of Marriage

Adam was overjoyed as he received this woman from God. He cried out:

- *"This is now bone of my bones and flesh of my flesh; she shall be called 'woman' for she was taken out of man."*
- *For this reason a man will leave his father and mother and be united to his wife, and they will become one flesh (Genesis 2:23, 24).*

Thus began the basis for marriage, which has been instituted and designed by God from the very beginning of time. A marriage consists of one man and one woman who will leave their parents and cleave unto one another. Together, the two become one. The institution of marriage predates any other institution on the face of the earth. It is the foundation of all nations and peoples.

Jesus and Marriage

When the Pharisees questioned Jesus as to the reasons for divorce, Jesus quoted from the second chapter of Genesis adding:

- *Therefore what God has joined together let man not separate (Matthew 19:6).*

The institution of marriage is very important to stability in the home, the nation, and ultimately the world. It is under very heavy attack by Satan in our world today. If the marriage can be destroyed, then the family, the country, and the church will also be destroyed.

But there is another reason that Satan, the liar from the beginning, works so hard to destroy marriages. **Marriage is**

a picture of the relationship of Christ and his church. Numerous times throughout the New Testament the church is pictured as the bride of Christ.

- *I promised you to one husband, to Christ so that I may present you as a pure virgin to him. (2 Corinthians 11:2).*

If we do not understand this concept, we may never realize what it is that Christ really wants His church to be. We may not understand the great love Christ has for us, and we may not understand the salvation that we have with Christ. It is Satan's desire that this picture of the church be corrupted, and so directs vicious attacks against our homes.

Christ and the Church

Paul gives us a glimpse of this mystery as he writes to the church in Ephesus. This text is often used as a proof text for the way men and women should treat each other in marriage, but Paul says he is talking about Christ and the church.

- *Husbands, love your wives, <u>just as Christ loved the church and gave himself up for her to make her holy, cleansing her by the washing with water through the word, and to present her to himself as a radiant church, without stain or wrinkle or any other blemish, but holy and blameless</u>.*
- *In this same way, husbands ought to love their wives as their own bodies. He who loves his wife loves himself. After all, no one ever hated his own body, but he feeds and cares for it, <u>just as Christ does the church</u>—for we are members of his body.*
- *For this reason a man will leave his father and mother and be united to his wife, and the two will become one flesh.*

- *This is a profound mystery—but <u>I am talking about Christ and the church</u> (Ephesians 5:25-32).*

The Purpose of Christ, the Husband

Paul is not really talking about marriage here. He is talking about the relationship that Christ has to the church. The purpose of Christ from the very beginning of time is to prepare for himself a pure church, a bride clothed in holiness, and set apart for service to God. Christ is faithful to nurture and care for His church throughout all ages. One cannot imagine that Christ would ever abuse or mistreat His wife.

In the same way, a husband must have the same relationship toward his wife. He protects her, provides for her, cherishes her, respects her, and if need be, gives himself up for her.

The Purpose of the Church, the Bride

- *...to him be glory <u>in the church</u> and in Christ Jesus throughout all generations. (Ephesians 3:21).*

God created women to be suitable helpers for their husbands. A wife is to aid her husband in obtaining goals, assisting him with his work. The Worthy Woman of Proverbs 31:10ff is an example of this kind of faithfulness. She brought good and not evil to her husband all of her life. Her actions caused him to be known and respected in the gates of the city.

In the same way that wives are to bring glory to their husbands, the church brings glory to Christ. The church is given to Christ as His bride. The purpose of the church is to bring glory to Christ—to be His helpmeet so to speak. As the Bride of Christ, we will be vigilant to bring good and not evil to the name of Christ as we go about our daily lives.

Jewish Wedding Customs

An understanding of Jewish Wedding customs helps to clarify Biblical texts concerning marriage. Marriage, in the days of Jesus, underwent three stages before it was final.

Engagement
1. The first stage was engagement. This was often made by matchmakers or the parents while the couple was still children.

Betrothal
2. The second stage was the betrothal. This generally happened when the bride was twelve or thirteen years old and the groom was eighteen to twenty years old.
3. The betrothal was legally binding. It could be broken only by death or divorce. That is why Joseph was thinking of "divorcing" Mary, even though they were not yet married. However, an angel came to him in the night and told him not to be afraid to take Mary as his wife (Matthew 1:18-25).
4. The betrothal was made with the giving and receiving of rings.
5. At the time of the betrothal, the man and woman were called "husband" and "wife." Yet, they did not live together as husband and wife until after the marriage ceremony.
6. The betrothal lasted about one year at which time the couples lived in their own homes. The husband used this time to prepare a house for his bride.

Marriage
1. The marriage ceremony began with a wedding procession to the bride's house.
2. The bride was to be ready wearing her wedding garments.
3. After the wedding the procession then went to the

groom's father's house for the wedding supper.
4. Guards were at the door and would not let anyone in after the couple arrived. Remember the parable of the wise and the foolish virgins? The foolish virgins were not allowed into the wedding supper after the bridegroom had arrived (Matthew 13:1-13).
5. Guests had to be dressed appropriately with their wedding garments. These were provided to any who needed them. Remember the man who was thrown out of the wedding supper for not wearing the correct clothing? He obviously had refused to put them on (Matthew 22:1-14).

Our Betrothal

Our marriage ceremony has not yet come about. We are the "bride" of Christ because we have been betrothed to him. He has gone to prepare a place for us and is coming again to bring us to be with Him forever. At that time will be the wedding of the bride and the Lamb.

- *In my Father's house are many rooms; if it were not so, I would have told you. <u>I am going there and prepare a place for you</u>. And if I go to prepare a place for you, <u>I will come back and take you to be with me that you also may be where I am</u> (John 14:2, 3).*

We read of the glorious vision of John in Revelation as Jesus returns to receive His glorious bride, His church.

- *"Let us rejoice and be glad and give him glory! <u>For the wedding of the Lamb has come, and his bride has made herself ready</u>. Fine linen, bright and clean, was given her to wear." (Fine linen stands for the righteous acts of the saints.) Then the angel said to me, "Write: 'Blessed are those who are invited to the wedding supper of the*

Lamb'" (Revelation 19:7-9). I saw the Holy City, the New Jerusalem, coming down out of heaven from God, <u>prepared as a bride beautifully dressed for her husband</u> (Revelation 21:2).

It will be a time of great rejoicing and celebration. The pain and suffering in this world will be replaced with an eternity of bliss and happiness. We will be together with Jesus forever and ever.

Conclusion

- *But when they came to Jesus and found that he was already dead, they did not break his legs. Instead, one of the soldiers pierced <u>Jesus' side</u> with a spear, bringing a sudden flow of <u>blood and water</u> (John 19:33, 34).*

Just as Eve was born from the pierced side of Adam as he slept, the church was born from pierced side of Christ as He died on a Roman cross. The radiant and glorious church was brought forth with blood and water. The church, as the Bride of Christ is worth His very life. He shed His blood to bring it into existence.

... <u>the church</u> of God, which <u>he bought with his own blood</u> (Acts 20:28b).

Purchased with the blood of Christ, the church became His bride.

The marriage of man and woman is a picture of the marriage of Christ and His church. If the picture of marriage is corrupted, then the picture of Christ and his church is corrupted. If the sanctity of marriage is not protected, then it will be harder to impress the world of the relationship between Christ and the church.

Christ nurtures the church as a husband cares for and nurtures his wife. The church brings glory to Christ as wife brings glory to her husband and aids him in his life's work.

Just as a husband and a wife are one flesh, Christ and His church are one. Many people say they love Christ but have nothing to do with His church. However, there cannot be love for one without love for the other. Christ paid such a tremendous price to purchase His bride; how could we ever conclude that the church is not important?

The unity of Christ and His church is like the unity of a married man and woman. If we belong to Christ then we belong to His church, knowing that our relationship with Him is like that of a husband and a wife. His eternal love demands our time and loyalty.

Being aware of this beautiful symbol of Christ and His church, we must do all we can to preserve the sanctity of marriage in our own lives and in our nation. **Marriage is a living example of Christ and his church.**

Questions for discussion:
1. What did Adam find missing when he named the animals (Genesis 2:19, 20)? What did God impress upon him (Genesis 2:18)?
2. How was the creation of man and woman different from the other created things and then different from each other (Genesis 2:7; Genesis 2:21, 22)? When did man become a living soul (Genesis 2:8)?
3. Compare the birth of Eve from the side of Adam, and the birth of the church from the pierced side of Christ, i.e., the deep sleep; the side being opened; the rib, and the water and blood.
4. What is the major role of the husband according to Ephesians 5:23-30?
5. What is the major role of the wife according to Proverbs 31:11, 12?

6. List some ways we bring glory in the church to Christ as our spiritual husband (Ephesians 2:10; Revelation 19:7, 8; Matthew 5:16)?
7. List the three stages of marriage according to Jewish customs? How does this differ from our customs today?
8. In your opinion, are we, as Christians, married, or betrothed, to Christ? Discuss.
9. According to scriptures what constitutes a marriage (Genesis 3:24)? According to Isaiah 5:20, what does God state concerning those who would confuse the issues.
10. What does Hebrews 13:4 state concerning marriage?

CHAPTER 3

THE COVERING FOR SIN
Christ, the Innocent Substitute

The Fall of Man

In the third chapter of Genesis we come upon the terrible consequences of the first sin. The whole chapter is one of lies, excuses, and punishment. It is a disturbing look at the weakness of man, and the deceitfulness of Satan, contrasted sharply with the justice and mercy of God.

The temptation of Eve followed the pattern of all temptations of man. All temptation falls into one of these three categories.

- *...for all that is in the world, the lust of the flesh, and lust of the eyes, and the pride of life, is not of the Father, but of the world (I John 2:16* KJV).
- Adam and Eve had been warned by God **not** to eat of the fruit of the Tree of the Knowledge of Good and Evil. They

were told that the punishment for disobedience to that command would be death. However, the Serpent caused Eve to look more closely and lied to her about the consequences of sin.
- ***When the woman saw that the fruit of the tree was good for food and pleasing to the eye, and also desirable for gaining wisdom, she took some of it and ate it (Genesis 3:6).***
- ***For everything in the world—the cravings of sinful man, the lust of his eyes, and the boasting of what he has and does—comes not from the Father, but from the world (1 John 2:16).***

When Eve was tempted by Satan, she saw that the fruit of the Tree of the Knowledge of Good and Evil:

1. Was pleasing to the eye—lust of the eye
2. Was good for food—cravings of sinful man
3. Would make her like God—boasting of what he has and does

Satan tempted Eve in all three ways. She thought it looked good, was good for food, and would make her wise like God. She was tragically deceived by the father of all lies. After eating this strictly prohibited fruit, Eve convinced Adam to try it as well. That evening as God walked through the garden, they hid from him, now knowing they were naked. Punishment for this sin was swift and decisive—Death.

The Wages of Sin

We always shudder at the news of death. Though Adam and Eve had no first-hand knowledge of death, they soon found that it had two parts, both involving a separation.

1. First, they no longer had access to the Tree of Life. They began the aging process which would end in their physical deaths—the separation of the spirit from the body (James 2:26).
2. Second, and more devastatingly, they were separated from God.

The God who walked and talked with them would no longer allow Adam and Eve to live in His garden. That sweet hour of fellowship was now taken from them and they found what it was to be alone. They were sent away from the plants they had tended, away from the animals that Adam had named, away from the joys and comforts of home, away from the Tree of Life, and tragically away from the presence of God. God's warrior angels, the Cherubim, guarded the entrance to prevent their return to the garden. It was a fearsome and shocking sight. The loss of all they had known was staggering.

Innocent Blood

If that wasn't punishment enough, the shocking face of death was brought near when God took the skins of innocent animals to cover the bodies of Adam and Eve.

- *The LORD God made garments of skin for Adam and his wife and clothed them (Gen. 3:21).*

The finality of death lay in the animal carcasses before them; it was ugly and grotesque, and it was irreversible. The innocence of their animal friends stood in sharp contrast to their own guilt. They knew the animals did not deserve to die, but were killed to offer them a covering.

The realization was unyielding:

1. The horror of **justice** (getting what one deserves.)—Death.
2. And the relief of **mercy** (<u>not</u> getting what one deserves)—Death..

- *For the <u>wages of sin is death</u>, but the gift of God is eternal life through Jesus Christ our Lord (Romans 6:23).*

When we sin, the wages we earn are "death." Justice demands death. Adam and Eve sinned; they deserved to die. The animals did not sin; the animals did not deserve to die. But God in his mercy did not require the immediate lives of Adam and Eve. He allowed animals to substitute for them.

"Death" Blow to Evolution

Sin brought death into our world. If there had been no man to sin, then there would have been no deaths. There could not have been millions of years of animals eating one another and dying before the first sin of man. Before the flood, animals and man both ate vegetation instead of one another (Gen. 1:29, 30). Not until after the flood did animals and man became meat eaters (Genesis 9:3, 4). Death came as the result of sin in our world.

The Covering for Sin

Lest we be overcome with hopelessness in the tragedy of these deaths and the expulsion of Adam and Eve from the garden, we are given a statement of hope. We must not overlook the short and simple sentence in Genesis 3:21, which carries a stunning visual of the great love the Father has for His children.

- *The LORD God made garments of skin for Adam and*

his wife and clothed them (Genesis 3:21).

God did not send Adam and Eve into the world naked and exposed, but made provisions for them to be physically covered. These animal skins were a spiritual covering as well.

As a foreshadow of things to come, these garments of skins were a vivid illustration of the coming Christ, who was sacrificed to provide a covering for us. Just as the animals were substituted for Adam and Eve, Christ was substituted for the death we deserved; an act of justice combined with mercy.

Christ, our Covering for Sin Today

- *You are all sons of God through faith in Christ Jesus, for all of you who were <u>baptized into Christ</u> have <u>clothed yourselves with Christ</u>... (Gal. 3:26, 27).*

When we are baptized, we are clothed with Christ. This means we put on Christ like we would put on a garment. Christ becomes the spiritual covering for our sin. When God looks at us, he sees His Son, Jesus, covering us.

Remember:

1. The only way **into** Christ is to be **baptized into Him**. At that time God makes provision for our new clothing. Galatians 3:27 is such an important verse because it is <u>only one of two verses in the entire Bible</u> that tells us how to get <u>into</u> Christ Jesus. The other is Romans 6:3.
2. Christ died to provide that covering for sin which is required if we are to be in the presence of God.
3. The innocent Lamb of God has been slain for our sins and we are clothed with Him at baptism.
4. Now when God looks at us He sees not our sins, but

our clothing, the righteousness of Christ (2 Corinthians 5:21). His perfection clothes us and our sins are no longer visible to God.

Recall the parable of the wedding feast portrayed by Jesus in Matthew 22:11-14. When the guests arrived, one did not have the proper wedding garments. The Jews provided the wedding feast clothing for those who did not have their own. Obviously, this man had refused to put it on. As a result, the man was not allowed to stay. In fact, he was cast out! A guest who had been personally invited was thrown out for not having the proper attire!

The picture is plain. This clothing that God **requires** He **also provides.** This clothing is Christ, the perfect man. At baptism we are clothed with Christ.

What incredible **grace** (getting what one does not deserve) is provided to cover the sins of those who would come to God in submission to His will.

1. The clothing that I do not deserve, nor can I ever earn, gives me the gift of eternal life.
2. This clothing that I receive at baptism covers all my sin and presents me holy and blameless before God.

Conclusion

Praise God for His bountiful love and the marvelous mercy and grace offered to sinners. Just as He clothed Adam and Eve with the skins of innocent animals, He has clothed us with the righteousness of His innocent Son.

I have been clothed with Christ! My sins are covered.

Questions for Discussion:
1. Discuss the difference between justice, mercy, and grace. Consider this scenario: You stole money from the bank and were caught. If you received *Justice*: You would go to jail. **(Getting what you deserve.)** If you received *Mercy:* You would not have to go to jail. **(Not getting what you deserve.)** If you received *Grace*: You would be forgiven and given the keys to the city. **(Getting what you do not deserve.)** Give other examples.
2. List examples from the Bible of God's Justice (Genesis 6-8)? Can you give more examples?
3. Mercy (John 9)? Can you give more examples?
4. Grace (Romans 5:10)? Can you think of more examples?
5. According to Genesis 3:21, with what did God replace the fig leaves?
6. According to Galatians 3:27, with what does God cover our sins?
7. When do we receive this covering? What two verses in the Bible tell us how to get "into" Christ?
8. Compare the temptation of Eve (Genesis 3:6) with the temptation of Christ (Matthew 4:1-11) using 1 John 2:16 as a source of reference. Read this verse in other translations.
9. With what are we paid when we work "sin" according to Romans 6:23? Can we earn eternal life?
10. Can we sum up the gospel with 2 Corinthians 5:21?

CHAPTER 4

THE SEED OF WOMAN
Christ, the Victor over Death

God's Wise Plan

Penned by Paul as "the Mystery," while Peter used the phrase, "Things that angels long to look into," Preachers refer to it as, "God's Scheme of Redemption." They are all referring to God's wise plan to save mankind. Since the Garden of Eden, where friendship with God was broken by the first sin, man has needed a way to return to God's fellowship. And this plan was formed in the mind of God **before** the initial word of creation was ever proclaimed.

The first hint of this is in God's depiction of the serpent's future wounds.

- *And I will put enmity between you and the woman, and between your offspring and hers; he will crush your head, and you will strike his heel (Genesis 3:15).*

With a man-child who was to be born of a woman, God

would lift man from his fall and destroy the serpent with a fatal head-crushing blow.

Here is the first prophecy of the coming Christ in the Bible. Eve, not fully understanding this picture, must have hoped this redeemer would be her first born son, Cain, whose name means, "I have gotten a man from the Lord." What a shattering disappointment for her to see this firstborn, who carried all her hopes, become the world's first murderer.

God's Plan Unveiled

However God's ways are not man's ways. About 40 centuries later we find that God did keep His promise to bring the seed of woman into the world.

- ***But <u>when the time had fully come</u>, God sent forth his son, born of a woman, born under the law... (Galatians 4:4).***

God, in His wisdom, intervened throughout 4000 years of history, working with the family of Abraham, to prepare the world for Christ. No detail was too small to be left undone. Many conditions were prearranged to make the coming of Christ occur at just the right time. Some of these included:

1. The Greek language which was common to all nations.
2. Roman soldiers, who were present to keep peace throughout the nations.
3. Roman roads, which made travel easy and safe.

Thus, when these and all other things were ready, when the world was ready, God sent His only Son to destroy him who had the power of death, Satan, and to restore man unto Himself.

This son, born to the Virgin Mary, fulfilled the prophecies found in Genesis 3:15, and also in Isaiah 7:14, "Behold a virgin will conceive and bear a son." Jesus was that seed of woman portrayed from the beginning of time.

Satan, also, had been intervening throughout these years of history to prevent this seed of woman from coming. He tried many times to annihilate the children of God:

1. During the Flood
2. At the Exodus.
3. During the time of Esther with the evil plot of Haman.
4. With the vile killing of the Bethlehem babies.

However, Satan was not aware of the details of God's magnificent plan, and conversely he found himself as a major player in its fulfillment. With the birth of Christ, the prophecy of God in Genesis 3:15 began to unfold.

God's Plan Fulfilled in Christ

The life of Christ marked a turning point in human history:

1. His teachings amazed the people.
2. His miracles could not be denied.
3. He was a friend of the downtrodden; a giver of hope.
4. He attracted crowds of people.
5. He also made very powerful enemies.

Thirty-three years after the birth of Jesus, Satan watched with glee as the suffering Christ gave up His life on the cross. The murderous Satan was surely convinced that he had finally put an end to the promised redeemer of mankind and the promised destroyer of himself. He just "knew" he had snatched victory from God. He was basking in the thought that their long war was at last over. He was ecstatic!

God's Plan Crushes Satan

But three short days later, Satan discovered:

1. The crucifixion was not the killing blow to Christ.
2. The crucifixion was only an injurious strike to Christ's heel pictured in the first prophecy.

We can only imagine the tremendous battle wielded by Satan in the spirit realm to keep the Christ dead and buried in the tomb. But it was not to be. The battle was a total loss, and Christ, the seed of woman, would not stay dead. He struck the lethal crushing blow to the head of Satan with His resurrection from the dead. The prophecy was now fulfilled.

Since the children have flesh and blood, he too shared in their humanity so that by his death he might destroy him <u>who holds the power of death</u> — that is, the devil – (Hebrews 2:14).

From before the beginning of time, God's wise plan to destroy Satan was to be the death of Jesus on the cross. Not realizing this, Satan put Christ on that cross thinking that this death would be the destruction of our sovereign Lord. However, the power of His resurrection is the very basis of our hope. If Christ has not been raised from the dead, then we are still in our sins (1 Corinthians 15:17). If we are still in our sins then our payment for such can only be death (Romans 6:23).

This then is the **key** to Satan's power of death:

- *But each one is tempted when, by his own evil desire, he is dragged away and enticed. Then after desire has con-*

ceived, it gives birth to sin; and sin, when it is full grown gives birth to death (James 1:14, 15).

Satan has the power of death because he tempts us with evil desire, thus causing our death if we succumb to sin.

- *For the wages of sin is death, but the gift of God is eternal life through Jesus Christ our Lord (Romans 6:23).*

When we "work" sin, we are paid our wages in death.

Fortunately, God has placed limitations on Satan's power to tempt us:

- *No temptation has seized you except that which is common to man. And God is faithful; he will not let you be tempted beyond what you can bear. But when you are tempted, he will provide a way out so that you can stand up under it (1 Corinthians 10:13).*

Remember:

1. Satan twice wagered with God to take away Job's possessions and his health. (Job 1:9-11, and Job 2: 3-7.)
2. Satan also asked God if he could "sift" Peter like wheat. (Luke 22: 31.)

Our reassurance lies in God's promise to keep the temptations within our ability to stand. He will provide a way of escape with each one.

Jesus gave us an example of how to handle temptation. When tempted by Satan in Matthew 4, Jesus showed us the power of fasting and prayer, coupled with a working knowledge of scripture. This can give us, too, a way out of our temptations.

Christ's Mastery Over Death

However, our **mastery** over sin and death is only in the **resurrection** of Jesus Christ. God, in His foreknowledge, knew that man would sin, and provided the atonement for that sin in the body of His one and only Son. In the mind of God, Christ had already been slain, before time ever began. His death would provide the very way back into the presence of God.

- *...you were redeemed...with the precious blood of Christ, a lamb without blemish or defect. He was <u>chosen before the creation</u> of the world... (1 Peter 1:18-20).*
- *...the Lamb that was slain <u>from the creation</u> of the world (Revelation 13:8b).*
- *There is therefore now no condemnation to those who are <u>in Christ</u> Jesus. For the law of the spirit of life in Christ has set me free from the law of sin and death (**Romans 8; 1, 2**).*

For those who are "in Christ" there is no more condemnation. We are freed from the law of sin and death.

- *Blessed be the God and Father of our Lord Jesus Christ who has blessed us with every spiritual blessing in heavenly places <u>in Christ</u>. For he has chosen us in him <u>from the foundation of the world</u> to be holy and without blame before him in love. Ephesians 1:3, 4.* KJV

Spiritual blessings cannot be found anywhere outside of Christ. <u>The only way to God is to be in Christ.</u> Before the world began, God planned for those that would love Him to be holy and blameless. All it requires is that we be found "in Him," God's perfect Son.

Conclusion

What a marvelous plan to thwart the schemes of the Devil, to reconcile sinful man unto himself, and to satisfy the justice that sin demands! What matchless love God has shown us! He has planned for us a way back into his presence! Through the sacrifice of the perfect lamb, God's Son, Jesus Christ our Lord! This perfect plan— a mystery revealed by Paul and receiving the rapt attention of Angels— has now been made known.

Questions for discussion;
1. Where is the first promise/prophecy in the Bible concerning a coming savior?
2. List and mark two verses that show that God planned for the death of Christ before the creation of the world. (Hint: They are in the lesson.) Why are these verses important to know?
3. Explain how Satan has the power of death according to Hebrews 2:14.
4. What brings about physical death in our lives (James 2:26). What brings about spiritual death according to James 1:14-15?
5. What are some of the conditions that contributed to the "time fully come," in Galatians 4:4? Can you think of others? About how many years did God take to fulfill this promise to Abraham?
6. What limits does God place on the temptations of Satan (1 Corinthians 10:13)?
7. Did Satan realize that he was part of God's plan when he orchestrated, he thought, the crucifixion of Jesus (1 Corinthians 2:7.8)?
8. According to Ephesians 1:1-4, where are all spiritual blessings found?
9. According to 1 John 3:8b, why did the Son of God

appear?
10. What is the definition of love in 1 John 4:10?

CHAPTER 5

THE FLOOD OF NOAH'S DAY
A Warning of Coming Judgment

The Wickedness of Man

- *The LORD saw how great man's wickedness on the earth had become, and that every thought and intent of his heart was only evil all the time. The LORD was grieved that he had made man on the earth and his heart was filled with pain. So the LORD said, "I will wipe mankind, whom I have created, from the face of the earth—men and animals, and creatures that move along the ground, and birds of the air—for I am grieved that I have made them (Genesis 6:5-7).*

The evil upon the earth had reached a climax in the eyes of the Lord and He was sorry that He had ever made man. About 1500 years had elapsed from the time of creation, yet the whole earth was filled with sin and violence.

The picture was so bad that God brought upon the earth a cataclysmic flood which destroyed every moving thing. Three verses in a row emphasize the total and complete destruction.

- *<u>Every living thing that moved on the earth perished</u>—birds, livestock, wild animals, all the creatures that swarm over the earth, and all mankind.*
- *<u>Everything on dry land that had the breath of life in its nostrils died.</u>*
- *<u>Every living thing on the face of the earth was wiped out;</u> men and animals and the creatures that move along the ground and the birds of the air were wiped from the earth. <u>Only Noah was left</u> and those with him in the ark (Genesis 7:21-23).*

This tremendous disaster in the history of the world has not yet been equaled.

Worldwide Changes

Before the flood living conditions were mild and pleasant.

1. The temperature was moderate and constant. There was no need for special clothing or shelter, making travel over the earth fast and simple.
2. Man and animals were vegetarian.
3. A seed could be planted at any time of the year. Food was plentiful. There was a morning mist with no rain.
4. Life span on earth was very, very long.

After the flood living conditions became extremely harsh.

1. Weather was hotter, colder, and wetter than before, and changed every few months. Ice covered large portions of the earth. Special clothes, tools, and housing were

now needed. Travel was much harder.
2. Man and animals became meat-eaters, and wild animals were a danger.
3. Four short seasons presented themselves each year. The growing season for crops was limited to just a few short months, and the food supply became much more precious and scarce.
4. The life span was extremely shortened compared to the life span before the flood.

Conditions Today

The effects of the flood are still with us today.

1. Our food supply today is extremely limited compared to the food supply before the flood. At any time we could find ourselves a drought or war away from starvation.
2. Our living environment is not the same perfect one made for Adam and Eve. Our world today is vastly different from the original conditions that God created.
3. Our life is unpredictable and risky due to sudden and violent weather changes, such as storms, tornadoes, and hurricanes.
4. Our life span has been considerably shortened because of the sun's damaging rays.

The curse on the earth at the time of Adam's Fall in the Garden of Eden pales in comparison to the devastation caused by the flood. The earth will never recover from this world-wide calamity.

How Did This Come About?

This time period could be like the one referred to in

Romans.

- *For since the creation of the world God's invisible qualities —his eternal power and divine nature—have been clearly seen, being understood from what has been made, so that men are without excuse. <u>For although they knew God, they neither glorified him as God nor gave thanks to him,</u> but their thinking became futile and their foolish hearts were darkened... (Romans 1:20-22).*
- *Furthermore since they did not think it worthwhile to retain the knowledge of God, he gave them over to a depraved mind, to do what ought not to be done. They have become filled with every kind of wickedness, evil, greed and depravity. They are full of envy, murder, strife, deceit and malice. They are gossips, slanderers, God-haters, insolent, arrogant, and boastful. They invent ways of doing evil; they disobey their parents; they are senseless, faithless, heartless, ruthless (Romans 1:28-31).*

The sins so graphically described in these verses may very well depict the condition of the world before the flood. They may also characterize the state of the world in which we live today. These sins incur the wrath of God. Notice that they begin with ingratitude.

Taking the blessings of God for granted is very dangerous. Ingratitude leads to greed, violence, and ultimately a God-hater. As a result, depravity of every kind exists today, and the knowledge of God has been replaced with the arrogance of man. Peter warns us about thinking that this will go unnoticed by God and unpunished.

God Punishes Sin

- *First of all, you must understand that in the last days scoffers will come, scoffing and following their own* *evil desires. They will say, "Where is the 'coming' he promised? Ever since our fathers died, everything goes on as it has since the beginning of creation." But they deliberately forget that long ago by God's word the heavens existed and the earth was formed out of water and by water. By these waters also the world of that time was deluged and destroyed. <u>By the same word the present heavens and earth are reserved for fire, being kept for the day of judgment and destruction of ungodly men</u> (2 Peter 3:3-7).*

The message of the flood is obvious.

1. The flood is always used in the context of God's judgment upon sin.
2. The flood is a visual and catastrophic warning for us today.

We live in the world that has been ravaged by this global calamity. Our seasons change. We get cold in the winter and hot in the summer. We consult our almanacs for the planting cycles of food grown in our locations. Most of our grandparents die before they reach 100.

These are constant reminders that this is not what God intended in the beginning. As we experience these things, they should remind us of God's hatred of sin. They should also remind us that God does not let sin go unpunished. This is a world that has suffered a fierce judgment of God; it is a world reserved for judgment again. In the next judgment God will destroy the earth, and the heavens, and along with them all ungodly men.

Coming Judgment Again

- *But the day of the Lord will come like a thief. The heav-*

ens will disappear with a roar; the elements will be destroyed by fire, and the earth and everything in it will be burned up. (And now, the real question.) *Since everything will be destroyed in this way, <u>what kind of people ought you to be?</u> You ought to live holy and godly lives as you look forward to the day of God and speed its coming. <u>That day will bring about the destruction of the heavens by fire, and the elements will melt in the heat.</u> But in keeping with his promise we are still looking forward to a new heaven and a new earth the home of righteousness (2 Peter 3:10-13).*

Many nations have experienced a "Day of the Lord" which is a judgment of God upon that nation, but all of earth is moving toward a day of total destruction, one that will be by fire. This final Day of the Lord will come unexpectedly like a thief. Even Christ, the Son of God does not know the exact date.

- *No one knows about that day or hour, not even the angels in heaven, nor the Son, but only the Father. As it was in the days of Noah, so it will be at the coming of the Son of Man. For in the days before the flood, people were eating and drinking, marrying and giving in marriage up to the day that Noah entered the ark; and <u>they knew nothing about what would happen until the flood came and took them all away. This is how it will be at the coming of the Son of Man...Therefore keep watch, because you do not know on what day your Lord will come</u> (Matthew 24:36-42).*

The picture of people busy with their everyday lives before the flood is one in which we can see ourselves today. Therefore, we must watch and be ready because we do not know when this judgment will come upon us. It will come suddenly. There will be no more time to prepare.

But there is a way out..............

Saved by the Water

Ironically, the water that destroyed the world at the time of the flood is the same water that saved Noah and those in the ark. This pictures the water that saves us today.

- *In it only a few people, eight in all, were saved through water, and this water symbolizes <u>baptism that now saves you also</u>—not the removal of dirt from the body but the pledge of a good conscience toward God. It saves you by the resurrection of Jesus Christ (1 Peter 3:20b-21).*
- *And now what are you waiting for? Get up, <u>be baptized</u> and <u>wash your sins away, calling on his name</u> (Acts 22:16).*

God in his mercy has allowed us a way of escape from this coming judgment of fire.

The water that destroyed also saves. The water provides the escape. As in the days of Noah, escape today is also found in the waters—the waters of baptism. The water of baptism saves us. Don't be told otherwise. The verse states it. The water of baptism saves us by the resurrection of Jesus Christ. Baptism washes away our sins thus giving the answer of a good conscience toward God.

Conclusion

Judgment Day is no longer to be feared.

- *For the Lord himself will come down from heaven, and with a loud command, with the voice of the archangel* *and with the trumpet call of God and the dead <u>in Christ</u> will rise first.* (Galatians 3:27 states that those who are baptized are "in Christ.") *After that we who are still alive and are left will be caught up together with them in the clouds to meet the Lord in the air. And so we will be with the Lord forever. Therefore comfort one another with these words. (1Thessalonians 4:16-18).*

Those outside of Christ will not be ready when this unparalleled day comes. The flood in the days of Noah serves as a lesson for us today. God will not only punish the ungodly; He will also dramatically save those who obey him. On that great and awesome day those in Christ will escape the coming judgment of fire. They will be caught up in the clouds to meet Him. They will be together with the Lord forever. This is a great comfort.

The flood has always been a frightening picture of a God who judges sin. The changes on earth after the flood remind us today of the hatred that God has for sin. However, knowing that the water of baptism saves us, we can face the day with a peace known only to those who are ready. For those of us "in Christ," this will not be a day of great fear, but one of great rejoicing.

The flood in the days of Noah was a warning of judgment to come. Are you ready?

Questions for discussion:
1. How did God punish Adam after The Fall according to Genesis 3:17-19? What lesson should we recall each time we see or pull a weed?
2. What were the conditions on the earth 100 years before the flood (Genesis 6:5, 6)?
3. What begins the downhill slide of sin in Romans 1:21? List the sins that follow in verses 28-31. Do

we see these sins in our day and time?
4. With what did God destroy the world in the days of Noah (2 Peter 3:3-7)? With what will God destroy the world in the future (2 Peter 3:10-13)?
5. Through what was Noah saved (1 Peter 3:20)? How can we be saved from the coming judgment (1 Peter 3:21)?
6. According to 1 Thessalonians 4:13-18, list the things that will happen on the Day of Judgment?
7. Can we predict the Day of Judgment? Who knows when this day will come (Matthew 24:36-42)? According to these verses what should we do?
8. What are some of the great physical changes that have occurred on the earth since the flood (Genesis 9:22)? What was the reason for the rainbow (Genesis 9:12-16)?
9. Should we fear the coming judgment (1 Thessalonians 4:13-18; 2 Thessalonians 1:7-10)?
10. What did Paul tell the Philippian church would happen on the last day (Philippians 2; 9-11)?

CHAPTER 6

THE ARK OF NOAH
The church of Christ

The Ark on Ararat

Most major cultures in the world have a flood legend. Today, approximately 4500 years after this catastrophe, the flood is still a popular subject for books, movies, and songs.

Noah's Ark has been the focus of many search expeditions. In the last century many have claimed to have found the Ark on Mount Ararat in present day Turkey. Some have asserted that it is in pieces on top of the mountain, while others maintain it is buried in the foothills of Mount Ararat. However much of the information is speculative. Maybe God never intended the ark to be found. Human nature, as it is, would probably worship the Ark itself, instead of turning to God who had it made.

Noah's Plans for the Ark

The Ark built by Noah is a striking picture of the church built by Christ. The similarities are not accidental. The Ark is a detailed window into the church of Christ.

Construction aspects we have concerning the Ark are found in Genesis chapter 6. The blueprints for the Ark were given to Noah, who had never before seen rain. God was very specific in his instructions.

- *So make yourself an ark of cyprus (gopher KJV) wood; <u>make rooms in it</u> and coat it with pitch inside and out. This is how you are to build it: The ark is to be 450 feet long, 75 feet wide and 45 feet high. Make a roof (<u>window</u> KJV) for it and finish the ark to within 18 inches of the top. Put a <u>door</u> in the side of the ark and make lower, middle and upper decks (Genesis 6:14-16).*
- *But I will establish my <u>covenant</u> with you, and you will enter the ark (Genesis 6:18).*
- *Noah did everything just as God commanded him (Genesis 6:22).*

The world at that time was destined for destruction. Noah was given detailed plans for building the Ark so that the violent waters of the flood could not destroy those inside. The strength of the Ark lay in the fact that Noah was given the word of God, a covenant, to take them safely through the waters. The strength of the Ark also lay in the obedience of Noah to build it according to the pattern that God had given him. Noah had 120 years to build the ark.

Christ's Plans for His Church

The world we know today is also destined for destruction (2 Peter 3:6, 7). This time it will be a destruction of fire.

Christ, too, has detailed plans for building His church so that the very gates of Hell could not prevail against it.

- *Simon Peter answered, "You are the Christ, the Son of the living God. Jesus replied...Upon this rock, <u>I will build my church and the gates of Hades will not overcome it</u> (Matthew 16:16-18).*

The church built by Christ will survive even though the gates of Hell will try to overcome. He has sealed the New Covenant with His blood (Matthew 26:28). The strength of the church lies in the fact that Christ **is** the Word of God, our new covenant.

The strength of the church also lies in our obedience to do exactly as we have been commanded.

Instructions for the church are written to Christians in the New Testament. We are told to follow this pattern of sound teaching (2 Timothy 1:13). As members of the church, we must all do our part to see that we follow the pattern of God. Although Noah was told when the judgment would occur, we are not told when judgment will come again.

The Ark and the Church

Light

Noah was told to put a window in the top. Noah and his family could not see out the window at the landscape below. They could only look up to see the light coming in.

- *Make a roof (<u>window</u> KJV) for it and finish the ark to within 18 inches of top of it (Genesis 6:16).*

Jesus is the light.

- *When Jesus spoke again to the people, he said, "I am the light of the world. Whoever follows me will never walk in darkness, but will have the light of life (John 8:12).*

We look up to Him to light the way. As our light, He dispels the darkness in our lives, and guides us toward heaven.

One Door
- *Put a door in the side of the ark... (Genesis 6:16)*

Noah was to make one door in the side of the ark for all who would enter. There was no other way inside.

- *Jesus said again, "I tell you the truth. I am the gate (door KJV) for the sheep (John 10:7).*

Jesus, too, made provisions for the door, and that door was His own body. There is no other way inside but through Him. All who enter must go through Him as that door. There is no other way to get into the church, but through Jesus.

Those Inside
Those in the Ark were saved from the judgment of water.

- *By faith Noah, when warned about things not yet seen, in holy fear built an ark to save his family (Hebrew 11:7).*

Although no one at that time believed Noah, he saved the people he loved the most. **Noah saved his family.** What an incredible reward for obedience. Noah did not question God. He did not adhere to the philosophies of men. Water in those days came up out of the ground, never down from the sky. Yet Noah trusted and obeyed. He built the Ark and went inside.

In the same way, those inside the church will be saved from the judgment of fire.

- *For the husband is the head of the wife as Christ is the head of the <u>church,</u> his body, of which he is <u>the Savior</u> (Ephesians 5:23).*

A way has been provided for our escape when the world will again be judged. We cannot trust the philosophies of men. Just as the Ark was Noah's safety and refuge from the flood, our safety and refuge is the church, which is the body of Christ. As the Savior, Christ will save those who are in His body, which is his church. Like Noah, the story of our salvation will also be one of obedience to the commands of God.

Those Outside

All that were outside the ark were lost. Only eight people in the ark were saved from the flood.

- *Every living thing on the face of the earth was wiped out; men and animals and the creatures that move along the ground and the birds of the air were wiped from the earth. Only Noah was left, and those with him in the ark (Genesis 7:23).*

There is no promise of salvation to any who are outside of the church. Christ is said to be the savior only of His church (Ephesians 5:23). Those saved are in the church. The scriptures are very clear that the unrighteous will be held for judgment.

- *...the Lord knows how to...hold the unrighteous for the day of judgment... (2 Peter 2:9).*

A New Creation

After the flood, the world was again new. Those in the Ark began a different life on earth. The planet had undergone a great change. All creatures except those in the ark had been destroyed. As Noah and his family emerged from the Ark, God made a covenant with them that the world would never again be destroyed by water. Without this promise they would probably have feared each time rains came. Thus the reason for the beautiful rainbow we see even to this day after a rain.

- *I will remember my covenant between me and you and all living creatures of every kind. Never again will the waters become a flood to destroy all life (Genesis 9:15).*

God has also promised us a new heaven and a new earth after his judgment of fire. The world as we know it now will no longer exist, and a new dwelling, a place of righteousness will be ready for us.

- *But in keeping with his promise we are looking forward to a new heaven and a new earth, the home of righteousness (2 Peter 3:13).*

Conclusion

We must make every effort to be found in the church on that day. I am not talking about the church building of course, but in the body of our Lord and Savior Jesus Christ (Ephesians 1:22, 23). Our families and our very own souls depend on it.

- *So then dear friends, since you are looking forward to this, make every effort to be found spotless, blameless and at peace with him (2 Peter 3:14).*

As we face the coming judgment of God, the church of Christ is the only place of refuge in which we can be safe.

Just as the Ark carried those inside through the storm and to safety in a new world, so the church will carry us through the storms of life and to safety in a new world prepared for us that love and obey the Lord.

The Ark is a brilliant window looking into the church of Christ. To be saved from the coming judgment, we must be inside.

Questions for discussion:
1. Explain Noah's trust in God rather than relying on the philosophy of the men of his day—(Genesis 2:5, 6) water comes up from the ground, not down from the sky. What lesson is there for us today (1 Corinthians 2:6, 7)?
2. How did Noah comply with the commands of God concerning the building of the ark (Genesis 6:22)? How are we to comply with the instructions of God today (2 Timothy 1:13)?
3. What comparison is there with Christ to one door in which to enter the ark (John 10:7-9)?
4. What comparison is there with Christ and the window in the top of the ark (John 8:12)?
5. What comparison is there with the church and those inside the ark (Genesis 6:23; Ephesians 5:23)?
6. What comparison is there with those outside the ark with those outside the church (Genesis 6:23; 2 Peter 2:9)?
7. If we all, like Noah, saved our own families, who would be lost? Does it make sense to neglect our own families while we seek to save others?
8. After the flood, a new way of life came upon the earth. What is the promise to those who are caught up with Christ in the coming judgment (2 Peter 3:13)?

9. Who shut the door to the ark after Noah and the animals had entered (Genesis 7:16)? Who keeps us by His power (John 10:28-30)?
10. As we wait for the coming of the Lord, some scoff and say that everything goes on as always, but what is the purpose for the patience of the Lord according to 2 Peter 3:15?

CHAPTER 7

THREE PROMISES TO ABRAHAM
Promises Fulfilled

After the Flood

Genesis is a most ancient and awesome book. The book of Genesis, which means beginning, is truly the foundation for all that has happened in our world. It records the beginning of all created things, the beginning of sin and death, the beginning of God's plan to save man, and indeed the beginning of a new way of life for the survivors of the flood. Only eight people had a remembrance of the world that had been. Those born after the flood must have had a difficult time conceiving that the world had ever been any different.

However, in short time, man once again returned to his old ways of defiance against God. In an attempt to predict the future and to appease and control the forces of nature, idolatry spread over the earth. Worship of the only true God was replaced with the worship of the heavens and other created things.

The Table of Nations

In Genesis chapters 10 and 11 (turn to the chapters as we discuss this part) we have a record of the sons of Noah and the destinations of their families.

1. The TABLE OF NATIONS in Genesis Chapter 10 gives the early history of all the families on earth today.
2. In this chapter we find the beginnings of powerful ancient civilizations.
3. In this chapter we have an astounding reading of the names of the first kings, and the nations that they founded.

Don't get bogged down in reading all these unfamiliar names. Just realize that these are the names of actual people; people historically equivalent to Alexander the Great and Julius Caesar. Herein lays the abbreviated story of how they lived, and the circumstances that initiated the passage of life as we know it today. This is the history of the beginning of nations. Read it with respect and awe.

The Tower of Babel

In Chapter 11 the story of the Tower of Babel is a tale of man's arrogant defiance and incredible conceit. The willfulness and pride of this group has had a devastating impact on the world that continues to this day.

1. Speaking the one language of God, the people who settled in the plain of Shinar decided to stay together and build a tower to heavens (vs.1).
2. Claiming to give glory to God by building a tower to

the heavens, they really wanted to make a name for themselves (vs.4).
3. Worship of the stars may have inspired them to build this tower. Possibly the tower top was "The Heavens." Ancient sources inform us of the practice of painting the zodiac on the ceilings of these structures (vs.5).

When God "came down" to "see" this tower to heaven, He was extremely displeased with the rebellion of man. A people so united would be a tremendous threat to others if their plans went against those of God's. In a boldly decisive move, God confused the languages of the people.

1. Families, friends, and coworkers could no longer understand one another.
2. Bewilderment and frustration quickly gave way to suspicion and fear.
3. The tower was named Babel, meaning confusion.
4. The city was abandoned as people regrouped and huddled according to their common languages. The Lord then scattered them to all parts of the world.
5. Like the upheaval of nature during the flood, there was now an upheaval of people as they searched for those who shared their language. Great danger and peril would mark these times.

The confusion of languages was another calamity in the history of man that still impacts us today. Our present world is segmented and divided because of this act of God upon mankind. The lack of a common language hinders research, progress, peace, and understanding.

The language barrier is also a reminder that a truly united mankind (one world government) will attempt to dethrone God and become a formidable threat to humanity. The diversity of language today is a continual reminder to society that God hates sin.

The Call of Abraham

At this point the plan of God narrows considerably in choosing one man, Abram, to bring the promised savior into the world. Abram appears rather suddenly in the genealogies of Shem, the son of Noah. We are not told any of the reasons that God would choose this one man to be the ancestor of Christ. But the fact that God loved Abram intensely is noted throughout the story of his life. When he is first introduced, the passage goes straight to the plot. In a remarkable conversation, God makes three promises to Abram.

- *"Leave your country, your people, and your father's household and go to the <u>land</u> I will show you. I will make you into a <u>great nation</u>...and <u>all peoples on earth will be blessed through you</u> (Genesis 12:1-3).*

    1. The first promise was that God would give him a land.
    2. The second was to make him into a great nation.
    3. The third was that the whole world would be blessed through him.

Abram and Sarai, although having no children of their own, were to leave Ur of the Chaldees and go to a land they had never seen and inherit it for their children's children. Abram was 75 years old at the time and Sarai was 65. The thought of children had long since left their dreams. However, they packed up and left, and trusted God as He led them to the land of Canaan. (Canaan was a grandson of Noah, one of the sons of Ham.)

Once again, God appeared to Abram and repeated the promise he had made to him earlier. In this dialogue, God outlined the boundaries of the land.

- *On that day the Lord made a covenant with Abram and said, "To your descendants I give this land, from the river of Egypt to the great river, the Euphrates—the land of the Kenites, Kennizzites, Kadmonites, Hittites, Perizites, Rephaites, Amorites, Canaanites, Girgashites and Jebusites (Genesis 15:18).*

From the River of Egypt (which is not the Nile but a creek south of Gaza), to the great Euphrates River in Syria, the land would be the possession of Abraham's descendants. However, during this time Abraham still had no children.

The Covenant of Circumcision

When the Lord appeared to Abraham again at 99 years of age and repeated the promises a third time, the covenant of circumcision was instituted as the sign of this promise.

- *This is my covenant with you and your descendants after you, the covenant you are to keep; every male among you shall be circumcised (Genesis 17:10).*

God changed Abram's name at this time to Abraham, and his wife's name to Sarah. He had chosen Abraham's heirs as the people who would be a part of His covenant. They would be marked with the sign of circumcision.

This symbol of circumcision is also given to Christians today.

- *In him you were circumcised in the putting off of the sinful nature, not with a circumcision done by the hands of men but with the circumcision done by Christ having been <u>buried with him in baptism and raised with him</u> through faith in the power* (work KJV, or operation ASV) *of God who raised him from the dead (Colossians 2:11, 12).*

Our circumcision is the work or the operation of God as He cuts off the sin from our hearts at baptism. Our faith is in the fact that at the time of baptism this surgery is done to our hearts by God. Our sin is removed. Baptism is never a work of our own, but an operation done by God.

The Promises Fulfilled

The Great Nation Promise Fulfilled

Abraham lived and died without seeing the fulfillment of the three promises made to him by God. But he believed God and it was credited to him as righteousness (Romans 4:3). Over 400 years passed as God completed the first two promises according to His own time schedule.

1. The Promise of a Great Nation was fulfilled after 430 years. Much of that time the descendants of Abraham lived in Egyptian bondage.
2. Initially **70 people** set up residence in Egypt when they left Canaan to escape the famine (Genesis 46:26, 27).
3. Four hundred years later as they came out of Egypt we read that there were ***six hundred thousand men on foot, besides women and children. (Exodus 12:37).***

It has been conservatively estimated that at least two to three million Israelites left Egypt. If each of the men on foot had a wife and two children, this would make about 2,500,000 people. The Israelites entered Egypt as a family, but left Egypt as a nation. God keeps His promises.

The Land Promise Fulfilled

The land that was promised to Abraham was given to his children's children in fulfillment of the promise of God. God rescued them from slavery in Egypt and brought them to the land of Canaan. The Bible states they possessed it and settled in it. Though some may say that the land promise is being fulfilled today, the Bible states that it was fulfilled in the days of Joshua.

- *So <u>the Lord gave Israel all the land he had sworn to their forefathers,</u> and they took possession of it and settled there...<u>Not one of all the Lord's good promises</u> to the house of Israel failed; every one was fulfilled (Joshua 21:43-45).*

God keeps His promises.

The Seed Promise Fulfilled

The third promise to Abraham was that through his seed the world would be blessed. This was fulfilled about 1500 years later with the coming of Christ.

- *The promises were spoken to Abraham and his seed. The scripture does not say, "and to seeds," meaning many people, but "and to your seed," meaning one person who is Christ (Galatians 3:16).*

The real "seed" of Abraham was Christ. As is written in Ephesians 1:3-6:

1. All spiritual blessings are found in Christ (vs.3).
2. He makes us to be holy and blameless in the eyes of God (vs.4).
3. Through Christ (the seed of Abraham) we are adopted as sons (vs. 5).
4. Through Christ we have redemption, the forgiveness of sins (vs.6).

God keeps His promises.

Through the blood of Christ the forgiveness of sins is available to the whole world. This blessing to all of mankind is beyond compare. What a tribute to the faith of Abraham that his seed, Christ, would be the savior of humanity.

Conclusion

The remainder of the Old Testament details the specifics of how God fulfilled these promises to Abraham, and in so doing, completely satisfied the promise given to Eve in the garden. Christ, the seed of Abraham, was also the seed of woman (Gen. 3:15). Understanding these promises and their completion is a **major** key to understanding the Bible.

Because of the remarkable love that God had for Abraham he was chosen to be the Father of Nations and the Bringer of Blessings to the world. God was faithful to fulfill all that He had promised Abraham because He loved him. What a marvelous relationship Abraham had with God our Father!

Are you the kind of person to whom God would come and offer to bless your family; not because they deserve it, but because He loves you so much? I want to be that kind of person.

God has a tremendous love for you and me. He took Abraham as he was and made of him a mighty nation fit for the promised land of Canaan. This picture of God's faithfulness to Abraham throughout so many generations gives us confidence that He can take us as we are and make of us a mighty spiritual nation fit for the land He has promised to us—Heaven.

God is faithful. He keeps His promises!

Questions for Discussion:
1. In what chapters of the Bible will we find the begin-

nings of all nations on the earth?
2. What devastation did the Lord bring upon man at Babel (Genesis 11:1-9)? Are we living with the consequences of this today?
3. Let's review: Weeds, thorns, and thistles from the Fall, Seasonal changes from the flood, and Language changes from Babel. Do these still affect us today? What is the message to us in these disciplines?
4. What three major promises did God make to Abram (Genesis 12, 15, and 17)?
5. What was the sign of the covenant with Abraham (Genesis 17:10)? What is the circumcision that we receive today and why (Colossians 2:11, 12)?
6. How old were Abraham and Sarah when Isaac was born? How did Abraham feel about his body at that time (Romans 4:16-21)? Did Abraham believe God? What lesson is there for us today?
7. When was the Great Nation promise fulfilled (Exodus 12:37)?
8. When was the Land promise fulfilled (Joshua 21:43-45)?
9. When was the "Seed" promise fulfilled (Galatians 4:4)?
10. Who is the fulfillment of the Seed promise (Galatians 4:16)?

CHAPTER 8

MELCHIZEDEK, KING AND PRIEST
Christ, our King and Priest

Pictures of Christ

God spends considerable time opening windows for us in the Bible. It seems that if we don't understand the view from one window, He is more than glad to open another. He never runs out of patience with us so great is His desire to see us come to Him in knowledge and love.

Windows into the nature of Christ are abundant throughout the scriptures, although some are much more apparent than others. We have already seen Christ the Word, Christ the Husband of the Church, Christ the Seed of Woman, Christ the Covering, and Christ the Seed of Abraham.

In the story of Melchizedek, however, the image of Christ is somewhat hazy. In fact it is so blurred, that if we are not careful, we may miss it altogether. Very suddenly Melchizedek appears, and almost as suddenly, he disappears from the Biblical narrative. We would probably read about this great man and give him no more thought until we read about him in one of David's Messianic Psalms.

- *The LORD has sworn and will not change his mind: "You are a priest forever, in the order of Melchizedek" (Psalm 110:4).*

Obviously, there is more to Melchizedek than we originally realized.

We first come across Melchizedek after Abraham had defeated the kings from the East with his own army and rescued his nephew Lot who had been taken hostage. As Abraham came home, he was met by the King and Priest of Salem (later Jerusalem), who blessed him.

- *Then Melchizedek king of Salem brought out bread and wine. He was priest of God Most High, and he blessed Abram saying, "Blessed be Abram by God Most High, Creator of heaven and earth. And blessed be the God Most High who delivered your enemies into your hand." Then Abram gave him a tenth of everything (Genesis 14:18-20).*

These three short verses are the only history that mentions this priestly king in the Old Testament. If it were not for the writer of Hebrews, Melchizedek would still be a mystery to us. Who he was, from whence he came, and his importance in history would be lost to our ignorance. But he is such a significant part of God's portrait of Jesus that an entire chapter in Hebrews is devoted to this mysterious man. We shall turn our study to Leviticus Chapter 21 and Hebrews Chapter 7.

The Levitical Priesthood

To understand the superiority of the Priesthood of Melchizedek we must first understand the regulations of the Levitical Priesthood. The Levitical priesthood was in effect at the time of Christ. It had its beginnings at the time the children of Israel left the land of Egypt and began their journey to Canaan. At Mount Sinai God gave them instructions on how he was to be worshipped. In Leviticus 21 God instituted many laws and regulations concerning the priests who were to minister to him at the tabernacle. In Leviticus chapter 21 we find many regulations given to the priests so they would be eligible to serve.

1. The first and foremost regulation was that only those who were descended from the tribe of Levi (the third son of Jacob) could serve as priests. Of the twelve tribes of Israel only Levi's family was given this privilege of holy service.
2. There were many other rules about physical perfection, rules for cleanliness, and rules for marriage.

To be a priest of the Most High God was a sacred charge; one that deserved a most holy man. Unfortunately, these qualifications of priesthood did not go beyond the physical. The priesthood did not depend on the type of person the man was, but rather on his family lineage and outward appearance.

Throughout the history of Israel, the priesthood was vulnerable to corrupt men. Many men who met the qualifications of lineage and physical perfection were lacking in personal integrity. Often, the priests led the people away from God instead of bringing them closer. At other times, the priests were severely punished for their lack of respect for God's laws and God's people. Although the Levitical Priesthood, as an office, did have the esteem of the Israelite nation, it fell short in the area of individual virtue.

Melchizedek was Superior

As we read in Hebrews chapter 7, we find the author making quite an argument about the superiority of the Priesthood of Melchizedek over the Levitical Priesthood. His priesthood was based on his moral integrity alone, thus noted by his name.

- *...First his name means "king of righteousness," then also, "king of Salem," means "king of peace." Without father or mother, without genealogy, without beginning of days or end of life, like the Son of God he remains a priest forever (Hebrews 7: 2b-3).*

Melchizedek was observed as having neither father nor mother. In other words, his priesthood did not depend on his lineage. We have no record of where he came from or where he disappeared to in history. His priesthood also did not depend on any of the other rules and regulations to which the Levitical priests had to adhere.

The purpose of the book of Hebrews was to convince the Hebrew nation (the Jews), that Jesus was the fulfillment of all the Old Testament. The new covenant which God had promised had now come into effect with the death of Jesus on the cross, thus necessitating a change in the priesthood. The difficulty lay in the Law of Moses which dictated that priests be from the tribe of Levi. Because Jesus was born from the kingly tribe of Judah, the Jews could not comprehend that he could be their High Priest. He was from the wrong tribe! It would be one thing to consider Jesus as King, but quite another to render him as High Priest.

The purpose of the seventh chapter of Hebrews was to convince the Jews that there had been a change in the

Priesthood and that the Levitical Priesthood was no longer relevant. The author explained that Jesus was a high priest after the order of Melchizedek. Since Melchizedek was better qualified to serve God because he was righteous, then Jesus was best qualified to serve God because he was perfect. The author gives several arguments to that effect.

Jesus, Our High Priest

Hebrews Chapter 7

1. The Father of the Jews, Abraham, paid tithes to Melchizedek acknowledging that Melchizedek was greater than Abraham (Hebrews 7: 4-8).
2. Even their ancestor, Levi, paid tithes to Melchizedek, being in the body of his great-grandfather Abraham—so to speak (Hebrews 7:9-10).
3. Because perfection could not come from the Levitical Priesthood, from which the law had come, a change in the priesthood was necessary—one after the order of Melchizedek (Hebrews 7: 11-12).
4. Jesus was like Melchizedek in that His priesthood did not depend on genealogies (Hebrews 7: 13-16).
5. Jesus was greater than Melchizedek because He lives forever (Hebrews 7: 16).
6. Jesus was greater than the other priests because He was made a priest with an oath from God (Hebrews 7: 17-22).
7. Jesus was greater than the Levitical priests because He is able to save completely those who come to Him (Hebrews 7: 23-25).
8. Jesus was greater than the Levitical priests because He did not have to offer sacrifices for His own sin as the earthly priests had to did (Hebrews 7: 26-27).

- *Such a high priest meets our need—one who is holy, blameless, pure, set apart from sinners, exalted above the heavens (Hebrews 7:26).*

Conclusion

Jesus was made a priest forever after the order of Melchizedek. God instituted this change with a solemn oath, which was never done with any priest in the Levitical priesthood. With this oath alone, Melchizedek was shown to be greater than Levi, and Christ to be superior to Melchizedek. God paints Melchizedek, to whom even Abraham paid homage, as a picture of the righteous Christ.

This illustration of the obscure King and Priest in the Old Testament now takes on new meaning. We come to understand that Melchizedek had a dual role as King and Priest. Because he preceded the Law of Moses, he did not need to be from a certain tribe in order to inherit this role.

Christ, like Melchizedek, has the dual role of King and Priest for us who believe today. Christ did not inherit this role because of His family lineage. Rather, Christ is our King and Priest because of His righteous nature. He is holy, blameless, pure, set apart from sinners, and exalted above the heavens. Can this be said of any earthly priest?

Like Melchizedek, Jesus is King and High Priest. Therefore, He is able to save completely those who come to him!

Questions for discussion:
1. Where was Melchizedek a king and a priest? What does his name mean (Hebrews 7:2b, 3)?
2. What did Abraham show when he paid tithes to Melchizedek (Hebrews 7:4-8)?
3. What was the priestly tribe of the Jews? Could a

man be a priest if he did not descend from this tribe (Leviticus 21)?
4. Why does it say that Melchizedek had neither father or mother, nor beginning or end (Hebrews 7:2b, 3)?
5. Why is Christ not a priest after the Levitical order? From which tribe did Jesus descend (Matthew 1:3)? From which tribe did the kings descend?
6. How did the writer of Hebrews seek to convince the Jews that Christ was both King and Priest (Hebrews 7:11, 12)?
7. Give two reasons why Jesus as priest after the order of Melchizedek is greater than the priests after the order of Levi according to Hebrews 7:11-16.
8. Did the Levitical priests have to first offer sacrifices for their own sins? Did Jesus have to offer sacrifices for His own sins (Hebrews 7: 27). What did Jesus offer as a sacrifice for the sins of all men?
9. According to Hebrews 7:26, how does Jesus meet our needs as a high priest?
10. Why is Jesus able to save completely those who come to Him (Hebrews 7:25)?

CHAPTER 9

SARAH AND HAGAR
The Old and New Testaments

Abraham Believed God

- *And Abram said, "You have given me no children; so a servant in my household will be my heir." Then the word of the LORD came to him: "This man will not be your heir, but a son coming from your own body will be your heir." He took him outside and said, "Look up at the heavens and count the stars—if indeed you can count them." Then he said to him, "So shall your offspring be." Abram believed the LORD, and he credited it to him as righteousness (Genesis 15:3-6).*

Abram received three great promises from God.

1. God promised that his descendants would become a great nation.
2. God promised they would be given the land of Canaan.
3. God promised that through his seed the whole world

would be blessed.

He just had one problem. He had no children.

He could only suppose that God would make his servant Eliezar his heir. So Abram asked God if that was what he had in mind. But the Lord did not have Eliezar in mind, and assured Abram that he would have a son from his own body. The Lord further guaranteed Abram that his descendants would be as countless as the stars in the sky. And Abram believed God.

Where is the Promised Son?

- *Now Sarai, Abram's wife, had borne him no children. But she had an Egyptian maidservant named Hagar; so she said to Abram, "The LORD has kept me from having children. Go, sleep with my maidservant; perhaps I can build a family through her." Abram agreed to what Sarai said. <u>So after Abram had been living in Canaan ten years, Sarai his wife gave her to her husband to be his wife</u>. He slept with Hagar, and she conceived... (Genesis 16:1-4).*
- *So Hagar bore Abram a son, and Abram gave the name Ishmael to the son she had borne. Abram was eighty-six years old when Hagar bore him Ishmael. Genesis 16:15, 16.*

At this point Sarai took matters into her own hands. They had lived in the land of Canaan for ten years and there was still no child. Assuming that God needed some help with His promises she offered her servant, Hagar, to Abraham as his wife. This was a common custom at the time, and no one was surprised or shocked at the arrangement. Any child born to the maidservant would have been considered Sarai's child. Abram agreed, and from that union his first son, Ishmael, was born. But this was not the son that

God had planned.

Thirteen years after the birth of Ishmael, God came to Abram a third time to confirm His promises.

- *When Abram was 99 years old, the LORD appeared to him and said, "I am the God Almighty, walk before me and be blameless<u>. I will confirm my covenant</u> between me and you and will greatly increase your numbers" (Genesis 17:1, 2).*
- *God also said to Abraham, "...I will bless her and will surely give you a son by her. I will bless her so that she will be the mother of nations; kings of peoples will come from her." And Abraham fell facedown; he <u>laughed</u> and said to himself, "Will a son be born to a man a hundred years old? Will Sarah bear a child at the age of ninety? And Abraham said to God, "If only Ishmael might live under your blessing." Then God said, <u>"Yes, but your wife Sarah will bear you a son, and you will call him Isaac. I will establish my covenant with him as an everlasting covenant for his descendants after him..."</u> (Genesis 17:15-19).*
- *"But my covenant I will establish with Isaac, whom Sarah will bear to you by this time next year" (Genesis 17:2).*

Isaac, the Son of Promise

The puzzle is solved. The promised son would be from both Abraham and Sarah. Did you notice the reaction? Abraham laughed!! What seemed so impossible to him at their late ages was possible with God. Here we are treated to a glimpse into the humor of God. He told Abraham to name his son Isaac. Isaac means "he laughs." In the next chapter of Genesis we read that Sarah also laughed when she heard the news. But God laughed last.

- *Now the LORD was gracious to Sarah as he had said,*

and the LORD did for Sarah what he had promised. <u>Sarah became pregnant and bore a son to Abraham in his old age, at the very time God had promised him</u>. Abraham gave the name Isaac to the son Sarah bore him...Abraham was a hundred years old when his son Isaac was born. Sarah said, "God has brought me laughter, and everyone who hears about this will laugh with me" (Genesis 21:1-7).

After waiting 25 years for a child of her own, God finally opened the womb of Sarah. At 90 years of age she gave birth to their son of promise, Isaac. The time had come. The promise was fulfilled. Abraham now had his heir, the child who would beget many nations and kings. A child of Abraham and of Sarah had been born. There was great rejoicing. The impossible had been done. God keeps His promises.

Two Sons

- *The child grew and was weaned, and on the day Isaac was weaned Abraham held a great feast. But Sarah saw that the son who Hagar the Egyptian had borne to Abraham was mocking, and she said to Abraham, <u>"Get rid of that slave woman and her son, for that slave woman's son will never share in the inheritance with my son Isaac.</u> The matter distressed Abraham greatly because it concerned his son. But God said to him, "Do not be so distressed about the boy and your maidservant. Listen to whatever Sarah tells you, because it is through Isaac that your offspring will be reckoned (Genesis 21:8-13).*

Sarah felt threatened by the presence of Ishmael, the son of Abraham and Hagar. During the feast she found Ishmael teasing Isaac and decided she had had enough. She instructed Abraham to send them away so that Ishmael would not share in the inheritance with Isaac. Abraham, not knowing what to do, inquired of God and was told to send them away.

God assured Abraham that Ishmael would be the father of rulers and nations. So Hagar and Ishmael were sent away, and Ishmael became a mighty hunter and archer, marrying a wife from his mother's homeland of Egypt.

The seeds of jealousy and malcontent created by the birth of Ishmael remain in the world today. The descendants of Ishmael (the Arab nations) and the descendants of Isaac (the Jewish nation) are sworn enemies of one another. They have brought much suffering and death upon each other's nations. How sad that man cannot improve upon the plans of God, and that his effort only makes things worse

Two Mothers, Two Covenants

Our God, the great illustrator, gives us another view of His plan to save mankind. He takes the two sons of Abraham, one born of the slave woman, and the other born of the free woman, and compares them to the two covenants that He has had with man.

Our Bible consists of two main parts, the Old Covenant or Old Testament, and the New Covenant, or New Testament. Paul uses this Old Testament story to teach the church in Galatia that God had nullified the Old Covenant in order to put into effect the New Covenant. Slowly read these verses. They are not hard to understand.

- *Tell me, you who want to be under the law, are you not aware of what the law says?*
- *For it is written that Abraham had two sons, one by the slave woman and the other by the free woman.*
- *His son by the slave woman was born in the ordinary way, but his son by the free woman was born as the result of a promise.*

- *These things may be taken figuratively, for the women represent the two covenants. One covenant is from Mount Sinai and bears children who are to be slaves. This is Hagar.*
- *Now Hagar stands for Mount Sinai in Arabia and corresponds to the present city of Jerusalem, because she is in slavery with her children.*
- *But the Jerusalem that is above is free, and she is our mother...*
- *Now you, brothers, like Isaac are the children of promise.*
- *At that time the son born in the ordinary way persecuted the son born by the power of the Spirit. It is the same now. But what does the scripture say?*
- *"Get rid of the slave woman and her son, for the slave woman's son will never share in the inheritance with the free woman's son."*
- *Therefore, brothers, we are not children of the slave woman, but of the free woman (Galatians 4:21-31).*

The Old Covenant represented the Old Law which kept the children of God in a type of slavery, like Hagar the mother of Ishmael. It was associated with Mount Sinai where the Israelites received this Old Covenant or the Law from God. The purpose of this covenant was to teach this newly formed nation the nature of sin. It prepared them to receive the New Covenant later which would give them freedom from sin.

The New Covenant was associated with the heavenly Mount Zion in Jerusalem which is the heavenly city of God. This symbolized the church, established in Jerusalem, giving freedom from sin to all who were baptized on the day of Pentecost and thereafter. The New Covenant makes us sons of promise. We are no longer slaves.

Conclusion

Just as Ishmael was sent away so he could no longer adversely affect Isaac, the Old Covenant was done away with at the cross so we would no longer be affected by the law of sin and death. Hagar, the slave, and Sarah, the Free Woman, are compared to the Old and New Testaments of God. He has done away with the Old Testament which kept us in slavery, and has instituted the New Testament that we may live in freedom.

- *But the ministry Jesus has received is as superior to theirs as <u>the covenant of which he is mediator is superior to the old one, and it is founded on better promises</u> (Hebrews 8:6).*
- *<u>But you have come to Mount Zion, to the heavenly Jerusalem, the city of the living God.</u> You have come to thousands upon thousands of angels in joyful assembly, to the church of the firstborn, whose names are written in heaven. You have come to God, the judge of all men, to the spirits of righteous men made perfect<u>, to Jesus the mediator of a new covenant...</u> (Hebrews 12:22-24a).*
- *If you belong to Christ, then you are Abraham's seed and heirs according to the promise. (Galatians 3:29).*

As sons of Abraham, we are now heirs according to the promise.

- *Because you are sons, God sent the spirit of his Son into our hearts, the Spirit calls out, "Abba, Father." So you are no longer a slave, but a son; and since you are a son, God has made you also an heir. (Galatians 4:6, 7).*

With God as our father—more literally, our Daddy, we now have the full rights as sons. The Spirit which is given to us at baptism (Acts 2:38) is sent into our hearts and calls out to God our Father. As sons of God, we are also made to be heirs to receive the inheritance.

Just as Ishmael was sent away because he was harassing Isaac, the Old Covenant or Testament has been done away with so that we now have a New Covenant or Testament that brings freedom. We are no longer slaves. We are sons who are free!!

(Note) Remember that a testament is the same as a will. When a person goes to a lawyer to make decisions for settling his estate, the document is called the Last Will and Testament of that person. Legally, there cannot be more than one of these at a time. The Last Will and Testament can be changed any number of times before a person dies, but at his death ONLY the last one will be in effect. So, can there be ANOTHER Testament of Jesus Christ, as some religions will tell us? No, only the one in effect at the time of his death is legal and valid; any other is null and void.

Questions for discussion:
1. Compare Mount Sinai (Hebrews 12:18-20) at the time of the Wilderness Wanderings to Mount Zion (Hebrews 12:22-24).
2. According to Galatians 4:21-31 what mount does Sarah represent? What mount does Hagar represent? Which covenant did Hagar represent? Which covenant represented Sarah?
3. Why were Hagar and Ishmael sent away (Genesis 21:10-13)? Of what was this symbolic (Galatians 4:21-31)?
4. What was the law (the Old Covenant) powerless to do (Romans 8:1-3)?
5. What was the purpose of the old covenant, the law

(Galatians 3:24)?
6. When does a will or testament become valid (Hebrews 9:17)? Can a will and testament be changed after the death of the testator?
7. When did the New Covenant come into effect (Colossians 2:14)?
8. Can there be any other testaments of Jesus Christ? Why or Why not?
9. What has set us free from the law of sin and death (Romans 8:1, 2)?
10. According to Hebrews 8:6, how does the New Covenant compare to the Old Covenant?

Chapter 10

THE PASSOVER LAMB
Christ, the Lamb of God

The First Passover

It was not a good time to be an Egyptian. Darkness...locusts... boils...storms. The plagues sent by the God of the Israelites cast terror into the hearts of the Egyptians. As each plague defeated an (imagined) Egyptian god, the heart of their Pharaoh was hardened all the more, and he stubbornly resisted the command to let God's people go.

The last plague, death of the firstborn in all of Egypt, was the most dreadful. The only way to escape was provided by the blood of the perfect lamb.

On the night of the tenth and most awful plague brought on the Egyptians, God required of the Israelites a perfect male lamb. He determined to show not only His own people, but also the world, His awesome power and might (Romans 9:17).

- ***On that same night I will pass through Egypt and strike***

> down every firstborn—both men and animals—<u>and I will bring judgment on the gods of Egypt. I am the Lord</u>. *The blood will be a sign for you on the houses where you are; and when I see the blood, I will <u>pass over</u> you. No destructive plague will touch you when I strike Egypt (Exodus 12:12, 13).*

- *Then Moses summoned all the elders of Israel and said to them, "Go at once and select the animals for your families and slaughter the <u>Passover</u> lamb. Dip it into the blood in the basin and put some of the blood on the top and on both sides of the doorframe. Not one of you shall go out the door of his house until morning. When the LORD goes through the land to strike down the Egyptians, he will see the blood on the top and sides of the doorframe and will <u>pass over</u> that doorway, and he will not permit the destroyer to enter your houses and strike you down(Exodus 12:21-23).*

The instructions were explicit.

1. Put the blood of the lamb over the doorway and on the sides of the doorframe.
2. Stay in the house.
3. When the Lord sees the blood he will "pass over" that house and destruction will be avoided.

Imagine the confusion of the Israelites. What would blood on a doorway have to do with their deliverance? There was no way for them to know that God was portraying an image of the sacrifice of Christ.

- *At midnight the LORD struck down all of the firstborn of Egypt, from the firstborn of Pharaoh, who sat on the throne, to the firstborn of the prisoner who was in the dungeon, and the firstborn of all the livestock as well.*

Pharaoh and all his officials and all the Egyptians got up during the night, and there was loud wailing in Egypt, for there was not a house without someone dead (Exodus 12:29,30).

The Blood of the Lamb

The Lord is not someone with whom to trifle. There was not a house in Egypt without someone dead. The terror and the grief of the moment were enormous. The Lord God of Israel would not take "No" for an answer. His people were of the utmost importance to Him. He had a plan and Pharaoh was not going to stop it.

The perfect lamb, sacrificed on the night of the Passover, was a view toward his perfect Son, given for the sins of the world. Centuries earlier God had promised the Patriarch Abraham, that his seed would bring blessings to the entire world. Through the lineage of Abraham Christ, the perfect lamb, ransomed the world from sin.

Isaiah foretold this event when he wrote:

- *He was oppressed and afflicted, yet he did not open his mouth; he was led <u>like a lamb</u> to the slaughter, and <u>as a sheep</u> before her sheerer is silent, so he did not open his mouth (Isaiah 53:7).*

John the Baptist recognized it when he saw Jesus approaching him.

- *The next day John saw Jesus coming toward him and said, "Look, the <u>Lamb of God</u>, who takes away the sins of the world!" (John 1:29).*

Peter wrote to the saints about it:

- *For you know that it was not with perishable things such as silver and gold that you were redeemed from the empty way of life handed down to you from your forefathers, but with the precious blood of Christ, <u>a lamb without blemish or defect.</u> (1 Peter 1:18, 19).*

God Gives His Best

As we study the pictures of Christ in the Old Testament, one of the most outstanding we will see is that of the Lamb. From the time of Abel, the lamb has been one of the most oft sacrificed animals.

Here in the desert of Arizona we are fortunate to spend time watching the flocks of sheep as they are herded down from the mountains at the onset of winter. October through December is lambing season, and in just a few short days, the pastures are full of white, fluffy lambs, bawling and squalling and following their proud mothers. Often there are twins and triplets and, every now and then, quadruplets. They are so white, clean, and pure. We can immediately understand the concept of the innocent lamb.

Only the Best

Throughout the Old Testament, God demanded the best animals from man for sacrifice. There could be no defects, no imperfections, no diseases, or blemishes of any kind. The importance of this is of course the picture that He was painting for us of His perfect Son, Jesus the Christ. When the Israelites brought their diseased and imperfect animals, it angered God.

- *"When you bring injured, crippled or diseased animals and offer them as sacrifices, should I accept them from your hands?" says the LORD. "Cursed is the cheat who has an acceptable male in his flock and vows to give it, but then sacrifices a blemished animal to the LORD. For I am a great king," says the LORD Almighty, "and my name is to be feared" (Malachi 1:13, 14).*

The Lord never asked from us what He was not willing to give Himself. He asked for the best because He was going to give His best—Jesus, the sacrifice without spot or blemish; Jesus, the holy and blameless Lamb of God.

Celebrated in Heaven

The apostle John, in his vision of heaven, saw the Lamb of God who had been slain for the sins of the world. The four living creatures and the twenty-four elders were worshiping the Lamb.

- *And they sang a new song: "You are worthy to take the scroll and to open its seals, because you were slain and <u>with your blood</u> you purchased men for God from every tribe and language and people and nation" (Revelation 5:9).*
- *Then I looked and heard the voice of many angels, numbering thousands upon thousands, and ten thousand upon ten thousand. They encircled the throne and the living creatures and the elders. In a loud voice they sang: "<u>Worthy is the Lamb, who was slain</u> to receive power and wealth and wisdom and strength and honor and glory and praise!" Then I heard every creature in heaven and on earth and under the earth and on the sea, and all that is in them, singing: "To him who sits on the throne and <u>to the Lamb be praise</u> and honor and glory and power for ever and ever"(Revelation 5:11-13).*

Conclusion

The Son of God allowed Himself to be killed, and like a lamb, did not protest or try to defend Himself. He could have called ten thousand angels, but His kingdom was not and is not of this world. He purchased the church and men of all nations and peoples with His blood that was shed. Christ, the perfect Lamb of God, who came to take away the sins of the world, has completed His task and is now sitting on the right hand of the Father in heaven.

Just as the Lord, on that fateful night, "passed over" those who had applied the blood of the lamb, He will also "pass over" those who have been washed in the blood of the Perfect Lamb of God.

We have no fear of death or destruction. The Lamb was slain from before the foundation of the world, and has been proven worthy of all praise and adoration, both in heaven and on earth. He is called our Passover Lamb. For this reason He is honored in heaven alongside the Father.

- *For Christ, <u>our Passover Lamb</u>, has been sacrificed (1 Corinthians 5:7b).*

Christ, the Perfect Lamb of God has been slain. With His blood he purchased us for God. We have been bought with a price. Praise the Lord.

Questions for discussion:
1. How many Israelites had gone to Egypt (Genesis 46:26)? Why were they enslaved (Exodus 1:8-11)?
2. Using a Bible Encyclopedia look up the plagues of Egypt. Name the Egyptian gods that Jehovah attacked during the plagues.
3. The last plague was on Pharaoh, who posed as a god. How would this plague show God's power over

Pharaoh himself (Exodus 11:4, 5)?
4. How long were the Israelites to keep a perfect lamb in their houses (Exodus 12:3-6)? What were they to do on the 14th day? Where was the blood put on their home (Exodus 12:7)?
5. What happened when the destroyer saw the blood on the doorposts (Exodus 12:12, 13)?
6. Who is the perfect lamb that ended the sacrifices of lambs (John 1:29)? Who is our Passover Lamb (1 Corinthians 5:7b)?
7. How will we be "Passed Over" for judgment (Hebrews 9:14)? In your opinion is this an example of mercy or of grace (Romans 5:8)?
8. Describe the scenes in heaven in the following verses: Revelation 5:6-9; 11-13.
9. How did Isaiah prophesy that Christ would go before His accusers (Isaiah 53:7)? Have you ever seen lambs slaughtered? Have you ever seen goats slaughtered? (Hint: There is a big difference.)
10. At whose wedding feast will we be both bride and participants (Revelation 19:7, 9)?

CHAPTER 11

THE BLOOD OF THE LAMB
Life or Death

In the last chapter we looked at the Passover Lamb. Because the blood of this lamb was placed above the doorsills and on the doorposts, God "passed over" the homes of the Israelites. Thus, their firstborns were spared during the last plague on Egypt. The death of the lamb became a substitute for the death of the firstborn. However, the blood on the house was the sign to God that the lamb had died.

The Blood

Christianity has been accused of being a "bloody" religion. One particular group has gone so far as to try to take the "blood" out of their hymnbook to make it more acceptable to those in the world.

Why is it that God would make blood such a central theme in the Bible? Why is blood the foundation of His plan to save mankind? In this chapter we want to take a closer look at the blood.

- *For the life of a creature is in the blood, and I have given it to you to make atonement for yourselves on the altar; <u>it is the blood that makes atonement for one's life</u>. Therefore I say to the Israelites, "None of you may eat blood... (Leviticus 17:10-12).*

God has chosen blood to be the universal sign of atonement. Atonement is the punishment for sin that satisfies God. Blood, meaning life itself, is what He requires for payment of sin. And because life is in the blood, the blood belongs to the giver of life, God Himself. By disallowing the blood to be used for human consumption, God proclaims the blood of the atonement to be His and His alone.

We can identify the importance of blood to life. It is universally known that blood carries life to all parts of our bodies. Every person in every age of time has recognized that life is in the blood. Even children are aware of the fact that blood should be inside our bodies, and become frightened at the sight of blood.

Accounting for Blood Shed

Before the flood, animals and man had eaten only plants. After the flood, God allowed for a change in the diet due to the harsh conditions on earth. Meat was added to the food list. However, with this new provision of food, a caution was given to man. Man was to abstain from the eating of blood.

- *Everything that lives and moves will be food for you. Just as I gave you green plants, I now give you everything. But you must not eat meat that has the <u>lifeblood</u> still in it. And for your lifeblood I will surely demand an account-*

ing...And from each man too I will demand an accounting for the life of his fellow man. "Whoever sheds the blood of man, by man shall his blood be shed; for in the image of God has God made man (Genesis 9:3-6).

Because man was made in the image of God, man's lifeblood, meaning his life, belongs to God. No man had a right to shed the blood or to murder another. If he did, his own blood or life was required of him. Because all life belongs to God and is sacred, God did not allow one to live who had destroyed another's life.

The Blood Sacrifice

Sin was, and still is, very serious to God. The wages of sin from the beginning of time have been death. Blood has always been required as the payment for sin. Mercifully, the blood of animals was substituted for the life of humans.

- *In fact, the law requires that nearly everything be cleansed with blood, and without the shedding of blood there is no forgiveness (Hebrews 9:22).*

However:

- *...it is impossible for the blood of bulls and goats to take away sin (Hebrews 10:4).*

Animals were sacrificed year after year as a substitute for the sins of mankind. Their blood, poured out on the ground (Leviticus 17:13), could never be used for the purposes of man. The blood was the exclusive ownership of God showing that the life of the sacrifice belonged to God.

The lifeblood of the animal ransomed the life of man. This sacrifice of animals continued until God's plan entered the fullness of time. (Galatians 4:4). In fulfillment of the amazing redemptive plan of God, Christ died at just the right time. He became the perfect blood sacrifice to atone for the sins of mankind.

- *For you know that it was not with perishable things such as silver and gold that you were redeemed from the empty way of life handed down to you from your forefathers, but with the <u>precious blood of Christ, a lamb without blemish or defect</u> (1 Peter 1:18, 19).*

He foretold this in the Last Supper with his disciples:

- *Then he took the cup, gave thanks and offered it to them, saying, "Drink from it, all of you. This is <u>my blood of the covenant</u>, which is <u>poured out</u> for many for the forgiveness of sins." (Matthew 26:27, 28).*

Notice that Jesus "poured out" His blood for the forgiveness of sins. His blood "belonged" exclusively to God. In other words, the life of Christ belonged to God. His lifeblood was given by God and to God as a ransom for our lives. The blood of Jesus Christ paid the penalty for our sins. The death of Jesus on the cross, i.e., the shedding of his blood, is the substitute for our own sentence of death.

There must be a death for the last will and testament to become applicable. The New Testament or Covenant of Christ became went into effect at Christ's death. With His blood (meaning death) the New Testament was instituted.

The Blood-Bought Church

Paul advised the elders of the church in Ephesus to:

- *...be Shepherds of the church of God, <u>which he pur-</u>*

chased with his own blood (Acts 20:28).

With the tremendous cost of blood, Christ bought and paid for the church. There can be no higher value placed on any person or object than blood that is shed, especially the blood of Jesus our Lord.

The sacrifice of Jesus on the cross was the ultimate and final sacrifice for the sins of mankind. All who ever lived or will live can look to His blood for their salvation. God is not willing that any should be lost. However, if we do not wish to accept this sacrifice, we will find no other way for our sins to be forgiven. Only the blood of Christ can cleanse us from our sins.

- *If we deliberately keep on sinning after we receive the knowledge of the truth, no sacrifice for sins is left (Hebrews 10:26).*

There is no other sacrifice for sins. His sacrifice is the last offering for the forgiveness of the sins of mankind.

- *How much more severely do you think a man deserves to be punished who has trampled the Son of God under foot, who has treated as an unholy thing the blood of the covenant that sanctified him, and who has insulted the spirit of grace? Hebrews 10:29.*

At the time of the exodus, the Israelites put the blood of the lamb on the sides and top of the door posts. However, blood was **not** put on the thresholds of the Israelite houses. Very graphically the blood of Christ should not to be trampled underfoot. If we reject the blood of the covenant, there is no other hope for us. We have insulted the spirit of grace, and trampled on the Son of God.

The Blood of Jesus Christ

Shedding of blood is the only way that the penalty of death will be satisfied. The blood belongs to God, and only He has the right to require it. It is through His mercy that He does not demand our own blood for the price of our sins, but has provided a perfect sacrifice in the death of His only Son, Jesus the Christ.

The fact that blood must be shed and a life must be lost is horrifying to us who have been guilty of sin. But with amazing love, Christ paid for our sins with his blood, and now we are able to face God being cleansed of all unrighteousness. The blood of Jesus Christ plays the pivotal role in the redemption of mankind. Without it, there would be no peace with God. We would still be lost in our sins and worthy of death.

- *....Jesus Christ, who is the faithful witness, the firstborn from the dead, and the ruler of the kings of the earth. To him who loves us and has <u>freed us from our sins by his blood</u>, and has made us to be a kingdom and priests to serve his God and Father—to him be glory and power for ever and ever! Amen (Revelation 1:5, 6).*

Conclusion

The seriousness of sin, and the holiness of God, can only be understood in the context of the shedding of blood. A Holy God cannot be in the presence of sin, and we, as an unholy and sinful people, cannot be in the presence of God. The only hope for us is through the blood of Christ, which satisfies the penalty of sin, provides a substitute for our own blood, and makes us holy.

The view from this window is awesome. The shedding of blood that brought death to Christ brings life to us. **The**

prevalent message of the Bible is not one of punishment and death, but of forgiveness and life. Without the blood, there would be no redemption for mankind. Only the blood of Jesus Christ can wash away our sins. To take the "blood" out of the Bible message would be to take the very life from the Bible and render it worthless and anemic.

Blood is an illustration of life which belongs to God. Christ's blood shed (death) on the cross satisfies the penalty of sin for us. There is wonderful power in the blood of Christ.

Questions for discussion:
1. What command was given to Noah concerning the eating of meat after the flood (Genesis 9:4-6)?
2. What command was given to the Israelites concerning the blood of animals (Leviticus 17:11, 12)?
3. What command was given to the Gentiles in Acts 15:19, 20 concerning blood?
4. Why is blood to be poured out and not consumed by man (Leviticus 17:13)? What is done with a drink offering (Numbers 28:7)?
5. Why was blood not put on the threshold during the night of the 10th plague (Hebrews 10:29)?
6. Why is there no forgiveness without the shedding of blood (Hebrews 10:22)? Why do you think God chose blood as the avenue for forgiveness in all ages and all cultures?
7. How were we made to be a kingdom and priests (Revelation 1:5, 6)?
8. With what did Christ purchase the church (Acts 20:28)?
9. List the benefits of blood using the following verses: Colossians 1:20; Hebrews 10:19; 13:12; 1 John 1:7; Revelation 7:14, 15; 12:11.

10. With what was the New Covenant, the New Testament, of Christ instituted (Matthew 26:27, 28)? Can there be any stronger payment than that (Romans 5:8)?

CHAPTER 12

THE UNLEAVENED BREAD
The Sinless Christ

On the night of the most fearsome and dreadful plague, the Death of the Firstborn, the Israelites ate their dinner with their coats on, their sandals on their feet, staffs in their hands, and their bread unleavened. There was no time to wait for the bread to rise. At any moment the word would be given and the exodus from Egypt would begin.

At midnight the Lord struck down the firstborn in every house of Egypt, from the king to the prisoner and even to the firstborn of the livestock. In the midst of intense shock and horror the Egyptians frantically begged the Israelites to leave fearing that death would overtake them all.

- *So the people took their dough before the yeast was added and carried it on their shoulders to kneading troughs wrapped in clothing (Exodus 12:34).*

The exodus had begun, and this night was never to be forgotten. Each year the Israelites were commanded to celebrate this hasty deliverance from slavery with the Feast of the Unleavened Bread.

- *Celebrate the Feast of the Unleavened Bread, because it was on this very day that I brought your divisions out of Egypt. Celebrate this day as a lasting ordinance for the generations to come. In the first month you are to eat bread made without yeast, from the evening of the fourteenth day until the evening of the twenty-first day. For seven days no yeast is to be found in your houses. And whoever eats anything with yeast in it must be cut off from the community of Israel, whether his is an alien or native-born. Eat nothing made with yeast. Wherever you live, you must eat unleavened bread (Exodus 12:17).*

Leaven was a fermented scrap of dough, left over from a former batch, which permeated the new batch of dough causing it to rise. All leaven, was purged from the home, and no yeast was eaten during this time. The Feast of Unleavened Bread was celebrated for seven days immediately after the Passover remembering this time of deliverance.

The Symbolism of Leaven

Throughout the New Testament leaven is compared to sin and corruption. Just as a little leaven permeates the whole loaf and affects every part, a little sin can cause the whole group to become infected and contaminated.

- *"Be careful," Jesus said to them. "Be on your guard against <u>the yeast</u> of the Pharisees and Sadducees." ...Then they understood that he was not telling them to guard against the yeast used in bread, but against <u>the teaching</u>*

<u>of the Pharisees and Sadducees</u> *(Matthew 16:6 and 12)*.
- *...Jesus began to speak first to his disciples, saying: "Be on your guard against the <u>yeast of the Pharisees, which is hypocrisy</u>" (Luke 12:1b)*.
- *...Don't you know that a little yeast works throughout the whole batch of dough? Get rid of the old yeast that you may be a new batch without yeast—as you really are. For Christ our Passover lamb has been sacrificed. Therefore let us keep the Festival, not with the <u>old yeast of malice and wickedness</u>, but with <u>bread without yeast</u>, the bread of sincerity and truth (1 Corinthians 5:6-8)*.

The Last Supper

On His betrayal night, Jesus ate the Passover meal with his disciples. The meal was the same as it was the night of the exodus many centuries earlier and the bread had no yeast.

- *And he took the bread, gave thanks and broke it, and gave it to them saying, "This is my body given for you; do this in remembrance of me" (Luke 21:19)*

The bread without yeast symbolized the body of Christ. Just as the bread had no yeast, Christ had no sin.

Christ, the Perfect Man

Christ proved himself to be the perfect man. Though Christ was sorely tempted by Satan in the wilderness, he did not sin.

- *Christ was tempted in all things just as we are, yet without sin, Hebrews 4:15.*

As recorded in Matthew 4, Satan tempted Christ in the same three ways that he tempts all mankind (I John 2:16). Yet prayer strengthened Christ and enabled Him to meet each temptation along with knowledge of the scriptures.

1) Satan asked Christ to make the stones into bread—lust of the flesh.
2) Satan asked Christ to worship him in exchange for all the kingdoms he could see—lust of the eye.
3) Satan asked Christ to cast himself off the temple tower to prove he was the Son of God—pride of life.

Christ, on other occasions as well, encountered the same areas of temptation that all humans do.

- *For this reason he had to be made like his brothers in every way, in order that he might become a merciful and faithful high priest in service to God, and that he might make atonement for the sins of the people. Because he himself suffered when he was tempted, he is able to help those who are being tempted (Hebrews 2:17, 18).*
- *God made him who had no sin to be sin for us, so that in him we might become the righteousness of God (2 Corinthians 5:21).*

The perfection of Christ enables us to be forgiven. His perfect life substitutes for our sinful one. We are to never forget this act of love. Just as the Israelites ate unleavened bread each Passover to remember the exodus, Christians eat unleavened bread each Lord's Day, to remember the perfect sacrifice of Christ on our behalf.

- *On the first day of the week we came together to break bread... (Acts.20:7).*
- *For whenever you eat this bread and drink this cup, you*

proclaim the Lord's death until he comes. Therefore, whoever eats the bread or drinks the cup in an <u>unworthy manner</u> will be guilty of sinning against the body and blood of the Lord. A man ought to examine himself before he eats of the bread and drinks the cup. <u>For anyone who eats and drinks without recognizing the body of the Lord eats and drinks judgment on himself</u> (1 Corinthians 11:26-29).

As we partake of the Lord's Supper each Sunday, we are to bear in mind the tremendous cost given on our behalf. We must not take lightly the death of our savior so that we might have life. Our purpose in examining ourselves is not to determine whether we are worthy to take communion, for none of us is worthy. Rather, we examine ourselves so that we take communion in a worthy *manner,* which means we must always recognize the sinless body and blood of our Lord and Savior Jesus Christ, a sober recognition of the cost of our sin.

Conclusion

The perfect life of Christ purchased our salvation. His body crucified on the cross of Calvary summed up this faultlessness. Bread without leaven is a symbol of the sinless life of Christ. Communion with our Lord should never be taken for granted less we trivialize the cost of our redemption.

The unleavened bread is a symbol of the sinless Christ. He gave His life in our stead. We must always remember this as we take communion.

Questions for discussion:
1. On the night of the exodus from Egypt why was the bread unleavened (Exodus 12:8, 11)? Why did the

Israelites eat with their coats and shoes on and their staffs in their hands?
2. Why is leavening added to bread? Name items used to leaven bread.
3. List the commands to observe the Feast of Unleavened Bread (Exodus 12:17-20). On what day did this feast start (Leviticus 23:4-8)?
4. Of what is leavening a symbol according to 1 Corinthians 5:6-8; Matthew 16:6, 12; and Luke 12:1b?
5. At what feast was the Lord's Supper instituted (Matthew 26:17, 18)?
6. What did Christ say the bread represented (Luke 22:19)? Why was His body given?
7. What do we proclaim when we take communion (1 Corinthians 11:26)? What are we to recognize when we take communion (1 Corinthians 11:29)?
8. How was Christ shown to be the perfect man (Hebrews 2:17, 18)? List the ways in which Christ was tempted.
9. Are we tempted in the same ways today? Give examples.
10. Did Christ deserve to die for our sins (2 Corinthians 5:21)? What did His death bring us (1 John 4:9, 10)?

CHAPTER 13

CROSSING THE RED SEA

Baptism: From Slavery to Freedom

God's Promises Never Fail

The Israelite slave had a bitter life, and the return of Moses from exile only made it worse. In retaliation for Moses' and Aaron's request to let the Israelites worship their God, Pharaoh ordered the slaves to find their own straw to make bricks. The Israelite foremen were beaten and forced to work the people even harder because the quota of bricks was not changed. The Israelites became angry with Moses. In desperation he inquired of God and received this powerful answer:

- *God also said to Moses, "I am the LORD. I appeared to Abraham, to Isaac and to Jacob as God Almighty, but by my name the LORD* (Jehovah) *I did not make myself known to them. I also established by covenant with them to give them the land of Canaan, where they lived as aliens. Moreover, I have heard the groaning of the Israelites, whom the Egyptians are enslaving, and I have remembered my covenant. Therefore, say to the Israelites, 'I am the LORD, and I will bring you out from under the yoke of the Egyptians. I will free you from being slaves to them, and I will redeem you with an outstretched arm and with mighty acts of judgment. I will take you as my own people, and I will be your God. Then you will know that I am the LORD your God, who brought you out from under the yoke of the Egyptians. And I will bring you to the land I swore with uplifted hand to give to Abraham, to Isaac and to Jacob. I will give it to you as a possession, I am the LORD'" (Exodus 6:2-7).*

With one plague after another the Lord God of Israel showed His outstretched arm to be more powerful than any of the Egyptian gods. These mighty acts of judgment culminated in the death of the firstborn of all Egypt, from the firstborn of Pharaoh to the prisoner in the dungeon, and the firstborn of all the livestock as well. Only the firstborn of the Israelites was spared as they obeyed God's command to put the blood of the lamb across their doors.

During the night of the tenth plague, Pharaoh summoned Moses and Aaron and expelled the Israelites from the country. The Egyptian people also urged them to hurry and leave their country, giving them gold, silver, and articles of clothing. Six hundred thousand men on foot, besides women and children, arose quickly and with herds of animals and others set out for the Promised Land. Thus began their exodus from Egyptian slavery.

Into the Depths of the Sea

Following a cloud by day, and a pillar of fire by night,

the Israelites journeyed to Etham on the edge of the desert near the Red Sea. There they camped and the Lord hardened the heart of Pharaoh. In a rage, Pharaoh had his soldiers made ready and descended upon the hapless Israelites with 600 of his best chariots and his army. As the Israelites saw them coming in the distance, they were terrified and cried out to the Lord.

- *Then Moses stretched out his hand over the sea, and all that night the LORD drove the sea back with a strong east wind and turned it into dry land. The waters were divided, and the Israelites went through the sea on dry ground, with a wall of water on their right and on their left (Exodus 14: 21, 22).*

At daybreak the Egyptian army pursued them into the sea, only to be thrown into confusion by the Lord. As they tried to escape, Moses again lifted his staff over the sea and the waters crashed in over them all. Not one of them survived.

When Pharaoh's horses, chariots and horsemen went into the sea, the LORD brought the waters of the sea back over them, but the Israelites walked through the sea on dry ground (Exodus 15:19)..

The jubilant Israelites were ecstatic by such a miraculous rescue. With no visible way of escape, the Israelites walked through the sea on dry land. The Lord had incredibly opened a path in the midst of the waters. On the one side of the sea they were slaves, but after crossing through the waters, they were free men.

New Testament Baptism

Paul, in writing to the Corinthian church, made clear the

spiritual meaning of this act of deliverance.

- *For I do not want you to be ignorant of the fact, brothers, that our forefathers were all under the cloud, and that they all passed through the sea. They were all baptized into Moses in the cloud and the sea (1Corinthians 10:1, 2).*

During the act of baptism, through the waters, God made the Israelites free from slavery. In the letter to the Roman church Paul claims that through baptism God frees us from the slavery of sin.

- *Don't you know that when you offer yourselves to someone to obey him as slaves, you are slaves to the one whom you obey—whether you are slaves to sin, which leads to death, or to obedience which leads to righteousness? But thanks be to God that, though you used to be slaves to sin, you wholeheartedly obeyed <u>the form of teaching</u> to which you were entrusted. You have been set free from sin and have become slaves to righteousness. Romans 6:15-18.*

The "form of teaching" used in this passage is from the Greek word, *Tupos*, which means a pattern. We are to obey a pattern of teaching to be set free from sin. The pattern is the death, burial, and resurrection of Jesus. This is central to the purpose of God who had planned our salvation from the very beginning of time.

- *By this <u>gospel</u> you are saved, if you hold firmly to the word I preached to you. Otherwise, you have believed in vain. For what I received I passed on to you as of first importance: that Christ <u>died</u> for our sins, according to the Scriptures, that he was <u>buried</u>, that he was* _raised_ *on the third day according to the Scriptures (1Corinthians15: 2-4).*

We are not to obey His death, burial, and resurrection. We are to obey a *form* of His death, burial, and resurrection. We find this form perfectly duplicated in the act of baptism.

- *Or don't you know that all of us who were baptized _into_ Christ Jesus were baptized into his _death_? We were therefore _buried_ with him through baptism into death in order that, just as Christ was _raised from the dead_ through the glory of the Father, we too, may live a new life (Romans 6:3, 4).*

Baptism is the point in time in which we are freed from sin. We die to sin, we are buried in baptism, and then we are raised to walk a new life in Christ. Baptism frees us from sin to become slaves to righteousness.

This fact was further stressed when Saul of Tarsus met Jesus on the road to Damascus. As he was blinded by the light, he heard the voice of Jesus telling him what to do. He went into the city and fasted and prayed for three days. God sent a devout Christian, Ananias, to him, urging him to be baptized.

- *"And now what are you waiting for? Get up and be baptized and wash your sins away calling on his name" (Acts 22:16).*

Although Saul (Paul) had spent three days in prayer and fasting, and although he had repented of his sins in persecuting Christians, he had not been saved from his sins. He was still in slavery to those sins until he was baptized. His freedom from sin came as his sins were washed away in baptism.

Baptism: The Work of God

- *Therefore, there is now no condemnation to those who are in Christ Jesus, because through Christ Jesus the law of the Spirit of life set me free from the law of sin and death (Romans 8:1,2).*

What is the law of sin and death?

- *For the wages of sin is death, but the gift of God is eternal life in Christ Jesus our Lord (Romans 6:23).*

The law of sin and death is simple. If you sin, you die.

Only God opened a path through the sea to save the Israelites from slavery and death. Only God opens a path for us to be saved. Through the waters of baptism we are set free from the laws of sin and death, and made free to live under the law of life in Christ.

- *In him you were circumcised in the putting of the sinful nature, not with a circumcision done by the hands of men but with the circumcision done by Christ, having been buried with him in baptism and raised with him through your faith in the <u>power of God</u>, who raised him from the dead (Colossians 2:11, 12).*

Other versions use the words "work of God," and "operation of God" to translate this passage.

Baptism is the work of God. <u>Baptism is NEVER a work of man.</u> We cannot remove the sins from our hearts. We have the faith that God will do that at our baptism. The new life is one that is free of sin. At the time of baptism God operates on our hearts, cuts our sins away, and we are forgiven.

Conclusion

Our greatest need is for the removal of sin and guilt or our life here on earth will be a quick journey to death. Just as the Israelites were baptized in the sea and so gained their freedom from bondage, we are baptized in water and gain our freedom from sin.

- *<u>You, my brothers, were called to be free.</u> But do not use your freedom to indulge the sinful nature; rather, serve one another in love (Galatians 5:13).*

The baptism of the Israelites is likened to the baptism of Christians. It brings us out of bondage and into freedom.

Questions for discussion:
1. To what natural barrier did God lead the children of Israel (Exodus 13:18)? Who began pursuit and why (Exodus 14:5-9)?
2. When the people saw the chariots and soldiers what did they do (Exodus 14:10-12)? What did Moses do (Exodus 14:13)? What did God tell Moses to do (Exodus 14:15-18)?
3. What did God do to stall the Egyptian soldiers (Exodus 14:19-20)? What did the Israelites do in the meantime (Exodus 14:21-22)? What happened to the soldiers when they began pursuit (Exodus 14:26-28)?
4. To what does Paul compare this event in the New Testament (1 Corinthians 10:1, 2)?
5. According to Acts 2:38, Acts 22:16, and Colossians 2:11, what happens to our sins at baptism?
6. How do we call upon the name of the Lord (Romans 10:10; Acts 22:16)?

7. At what time are we set free from sin (Romans 6:17, 18)? At what point in time did we die and bury our sin (Romans 6:3, 4)?
8. What is baptism a "form" of? What is the definition of the "Gospel" in 1 Corinthians 15:1-4? What is the "tupos" or pattern for baptism?
9. What is God's power to save us (Romans 1:16)?
10. Now that we have been made free what are we to do with our freedom (Romans 6:15, 16; Galatians 5:13)?

www.ingramcontent.com/pod-product-compliance
Lightning Source LLC
LaVergne TN
LVHW041709060526
838201LV00043B/653